American Muslims

American Muslims

The New Generation

Asma Gull Hasan

CONTINUUM
NEW YORK   LONDON

2001

The Continuum International Publishing Group Inc
370 Lexington Avenue, New York, NY 10017

The Continuum International Publishing Group Ltd
The Tower Building, 11 York Road, London SE1 7NX

Printed in the United States of America

Library of Congress Cataloging-in-Publication Data

Hasan, Asma Gull.
    American Muslims : the new generation / Asma Gull Hasan.
      p. cm.
    Includes bibliographical references.
    ISBN 0-8264-1279-3
    1. Islam—United States.   2. Muslims—United States.   I. Title.

BP67.U6 H38 2000
297'.0973—dc21   00-060331

DEDICATION

To my mother and grandmother:
thanks for being tough, strong, feminine, feminist,
there for me, and everything I want to be.
Your life has been so different from mine,
and I want to fulfill your dreams for your life in my life.

In your light I learn how to love.
In your beauty, how to make poems.

You dance inside my chest,
where no one sees you,

but sometimes I do,
and that sight becomes this art.
                    —Jelaluddin Rumi

Contents

Acknowledgments

How do you thank someone for making your dreams come true? To me, every person who even listened to my ranting for one minute played a role. First, thank you, God. I know I don't pray enough, and I probably don't do what I am supposed to a lot of the time, but thank you for blessing me anyway. Second, I want to thank my family, especially my parents, Dr. Malik Muhammed Hasan and Mrs. Seeme Gull Khan Hasan. This book is the product of their emotional and financial support. They were such strong believers and contributors in my quest that sometimes I thought that maybe they should write the book!

My sister, Dr. Aliya Gull Hasan, and my brother, Malik Muhammad Ali Khan Hasan, have helped me on every level: from research to sharing their stories about practicing Islam in the United States. They are my muses. Other members of my family have given me similar psychic, intellectual, and grunt-work support: my uncle Dr. Imran Khan and his wife Dr. Shazi Khan, their daughter Sara, and my cousin Nadia Khan.

Many of my professors at Wellesley College should be credited (or blamed?) for my intellectual development. They taught me to take my ideas seriously and to assert myself—my thesis advisor, Ms. Louise Marlow, and my other advisors, Mr. Stephen Marini and Mr. Alan Schechter, among several others.

Most of all, I want to thank other American Muslims. Everyone I have worked with has been so giving and generous with their time: Ms. Najma Adam, Mr. Salam Al-Marayati, Ms. Zainab Ekbal, Ms. Shahmim Ibrahim, Dr. Nazir Khaja, Mr. Shabbir Mansuri. Their assistance was invaluable. I am indebted to Mr. Khalid Parvaiz for putting me in touch with many of these people. Also, even though he doesn't think men and women should pray next to each other, my uncle Adnan Khan along with his wife, Tina, put his chauvinist beliefs aside and used his ties in the California Muslim community to put me in touch with activists he knew.

Also, Mr. Don Lewis, though not Muslim, has been quite helpful to me, as well as Professor Derrick Bell at New York University School of Law. My editor at the Continuum Publishing Group, Frank Oveis, manages to be both sedate and rambunctious at the same time. Thanks, Frank for taking a chance on me and giving me my first big shot!

To my friends, and you know who you are (in fact, some of you are in this book—hope you don't mind), thanks for the memories! For every moment when you said yes after I've made a ten-minute speech and then asked "You know what I mean," I thank you. Your friendship means more to me than you will ever know, and, though our paths will diverge eventually, I will never forget you.

A.G.H.

Preface: *The American Muslim Dream*

Dear Reader,

John Lennon once asked us to "Imagine all the people, living life in peace." I am going to ask you to do something similar. Imagine about six million people who are Americans. Imagine that they believe in paying taxes and building commerce. Imagine that this group doesn't drink alcohol or consume drugs because of their beliefs in self-control. Imagine that they have to keep to a schedule allotting time to pray five times in the day as well as time for work, family, and enjoying themselves. Imagine a group of six million who believe in respecting women, specifically their rights to education, to consent to marriage, to divorce, to vote, to hold political office, among other things. Too good to be true? You don't have to imagine—this group is real. They are the Muslims of America.

My parents are from Pakistan, but I am American—an American Muslim. I was born in the Windy City (Chicago) and raised in a big small-town called Pueblo, Colorado, in the shadow of the Rocky Mountains. That's me on the cover on the right, holding my snowboard, and my sister, on the left. I am a self-proclaimed Muslim feminist cowgirl, a category I created. From what I've gleaned from a short lifetime of reading newspapers and watching television and film, I realize that most Americans would associate the word "Muslim" with black America and the Nation of Islam or with terrorism and certainly not with feminism or that most independent and self-reliant of women: the all-American cowgirl! At most 1 percent of Muslims could be described as terrorists and 5 percent as fundamentalists (although the latter term more properly describes a certain form of Christianity), but I am not one of them (and neither is the vast majority of world Muslims). My spirit is a mix of American individualism, the American West, the Islam that I grew up with and practice, my family's code of ethics, and the feminism I believe in.

This book is about other Muslims like me, who are living as Americans and Muslims and figuring out their spirit and identity as we all go along. The six million of us run the gamut in diversity: from a variety of economic backgrounds and practically every ethnicity you can imagine. Some of us are from the Middle East and the Far East, from Africa, and, like my family, from the Indian subcontinent, even Muslims from Vietnam and Cambodia (called "Cham"). A majority of us are African-American Muslims, as well as Native American and Hispanic, who have been here for generations—some as recent as last year from Bosnia and some maybe even before Columbus discovered America. Everyone in America has a dream, right? *The dream of six million of us is to be American and be Muslim,* and we're doing it. That is what this book is about. We speak different languages and have different cultures. Even though we're not all alike, we are all Muslim and American.

Some of us are quite famous actually. American Muslim Ahmed Zewail, a scientist and professor at the California Institute of Technology, won the 1999 Nobel Prize in Chemistry and Physics. He actually maintains dual citizenship in the United States and Egypt. His development of femtochemistry— the use of high speed cameras to monitor incredibly fast chemical reactions and very slow speeds equivalent to one-quadrillionth of a second, also known as a femtosecond—has laid the groundwork for the technology of the future.

He's not the only famous American Muslim. In fact, there are enough Muslim NBA stars to make our own all-star basketball team. One of the best and most promising basketball players today is twenty-four-year-old Shareef Abdur-Rahim of the Vancouver Grizzlies. Michael Jordan called him "A star of the future." Shareef grew up Muslim; his father is the imam at an

Atlanta mosque. He represented the United States at the 2000 Summer Olympics in Sydney, Australia. Joining him this season with the Grizzlies will be Mahmoud Abdul-Rauf, former point guard with the Denver Nuggets. Mahmoud, who suffers from Tourette's Syndrome, has taken some time off from basketball but will return to his former glory as one of the fastest and most explosive point guards in the NBA. He has an uncanny ability to sink every free throw he takes and even buzzer shots from mid-court.

Tariq Abdul-Wahad of the Sacramento Kings is another young Muslim player. He actually grew up in France, as his family is from French Guyana, and is the first French-born person to play in the NBA. He's called the "French Connection." He learned to play basketball from his mother who was a professional player herself. He was a star of San Jose State University and is known for his ability to play competitively and intensely yet remain composed and calm. Of course, we cannot forget NBA legend Hakeem Olajuwon. He is one of the greatest basketball players ever and a devout Muslim. Another Muslim basketball player is the Chicago Bulls' Khalid El-Amin.

This past summer, when I was in Beverly Hills, I saw Busta Rhymes, my favorite (living) rapper. I yelled out to him, "Hey Busta!" He said "hi" nonchalantly and headed toward his gargantuan SUV with his entourage of about three other men. Not satisfied with this brief exchange, I yelled out at Busta one more time: "*As-salamu 'alaykum!*" Recognizing the Islamic greeting, Busta popped his head back out from around the SUV and said in all sincerity the Islamic response: "*Wa 'alaykum as-salam.*" In fact, two of his posse also said "*Wa 'alaykum as-salam.*" This was very exciting for me. When I was little, there were no Muslim rock stars that I knew of—other than the tenuous connection that Simon LeBon of Duran Duran had married a model who was Muslim. The other famous Muslim I knew of when I was little was Muhammad Ali, who continues to be a hero to me and all Americans.

Some of the most talented hip-hop artists are Muslims in fact. Q-Tip of A Tribe Called Quest is Muslim. He is a pioneer in the hip-hop field and has been tapped by other artists like Janet Jackson to groove up their music. Other members of A Tribe Called Quest are also Muslim, as well as rappers Mos Def and Everlast and the female singer of Groove Theory Amel Larrieux. Some say that Tupac Shakur, probably my favorite nonliving rapper, was a latent Muslim, seeking solace in the Qur'an while he was in prison. On his last album, "Machiavelli," he raps that he's "kickin' lyrics like the Holy Qur'an." Originally from London, the former Cat Stevens, now Yusuf Islam, converted after nearly drowning on a Malibu beach. He now has recorded music about Islam and the life of the Prophet. He has even said that his songs about love outside of marriage are unacceptable to his Islamic beliefs, though many of his songs are acceptable including "Peace Train," and the classic "Morning Has Broken."

Even the landscape of America is changing. The architecture of mosques and Islamic centers has changed the way American cities and suburbs look, with their distinctive minarets and domes. This phenomenon has been noted by city planners as well as architects and historians. Some of our most prominent Fortune 500 executives have been or are Muslim: Faroowq Kathwari is the CEO of Ethan Allen; Atiq Raz is the former president of Advanced Micro Devices; Safi Qureshey is the former CEO of AST Computers. The Dow Jones has acknowledged Muslim presence by creating the Dow Jones Islamic Market Index (DJIM), which tracks six hundred stocks worth a total of $7.5 trillion that comply with standards of Islamic law (*Shari'ah*). The advisory board of the DJIM consists of scholars and judges from Islamic countries as well as a Muslim American scholar. Last year, the DJIM stocks gained 26.35 percent. Additionally, Muslims can invest in mutual funds tailored to Muslim interests or find mortgages that comply with Islamic finance practices.

You can live as a Muslim anywhere in the world. Islam, I once read, is as flexible as a rubber band—you can stretch it and keep stretching it, and it will never break. I like being an American Muslim—it is the right stretch.

Asma Gull Hasan
September 2000

A Note to the Reader

After invoking the name of God or the Prophet Muhammad, Muslims say a blessing. For God, Muslims say, *"Subhanahu wa ta'ala,"* which means Praise to the Lord. For Muhammad, Muslims say, *"Sall-Allahu alayhi wa sallam,"* which means "Peace be upon him." I have chosen to leave out these blessings in the text of my book so as to prevent any confusion on the part of non-Muslim readers and to preserve the flow of the printed words. For those readers who are Muslim, I suggest you say the blessing to yourself when necessary as you read and understand that my blessing was given as I wrote the text myself. The following is my opinion. I mean no disrespect to anyone. I ask Allah for forgiveness for my lack of knowledge and shortcomings in this and other endeavors.

—— 1 ◆ Mistaken Identity ——————

L
ike other typical American families, my family was
stumped by a "Jeopardy" answer: "The most common
name in the world," Alex Trebek read. We thought for a
few seconds. My mother then broke the silence announcing, both
hesitantly and with some boldness, "John!" When the "Jeopardy"
timer chimed, Alex stared down the contestants: "What is
Muhammad?" Alex then repeated in that ominous tone of his,
"What is Muhammad?" Normally, my family would move on to
concentrate on the next "Jeopardy" answer, or comment on how
unprepared the contestants always are. Instead, we were surprised by our own ignorance. Though the two males in our house,
my father and my brother, are named Muhammad, none of us
made the connection that Muhammad would be the world's most
common name.

If my family, which is Muslim, did not know this fact, how
many non-Muslim Americans would? How much do Americans
really know about Islam and Muslims? How much of what
Americans think they know is accurate? How does Americans'
knowledge, and more likely misinformation, about Islam affect
their attitudes towards Muslims in America and abroad?

The nuns at my Catholic school in Pueblo, Colorado, knew
enough about Islam to conclude that during religion class I
should be sent to the principal's office to study books on Islam my
parents had provided. I had partially brought this exclusion on
myself, however. The principal frantically called my mother one
day when I was in kindergarten. Though usually quiet—the
boldest thing about me was my big, brown eyes—I had

announced to my class that, contrary to Sister's lesson that day, Jesus was *not* the son of God and that God was a being who couldn't have children like humans could. That was what I had been taught by my mother at home, and, being a diligent student, I felt that I should point out when Sister was making stuff up.

Over time, I learned to respect what Christianity and Islam had in common. One day, when I was in second or third grade, I came home in tears, telling my mother that because we were Muslim, I would never have a hope of being cast as the Virgin Mary in the Christmas pageant. She reminded me that although Muslims do not celebrate Christmas as a religious holiday and do not have traditions associated with Jesus' birth, I could still enjoy participating in the annual Christmas pageant. Muslims do believe that Jesus was born of a virgin and that he was a beloved prophet of God. I triumphantly returned to school the next day, ready to try out for the pageant like all the other kids. I never did become the Virgin Mary, but when I was in eighth grade I proudly took the role of one of the three kings who visited Jesus' manger. As a religion major at Wellesley College, I enjoyed comparing the Qur'anic versions of Adam and Eve, Noah's Ark, and Joseph and his coat of many colors with the Biblical versions I remembered from Catholic school.

As I have become more comfortable living as a Muslim in a Christian country, Americans, however, seem to be more confused about Islam. In today's world, you would have to live in a cave not to have heard of Muslims. Having an accurate understanding of Islam on the other hand, free of media generalizations and prevalent stereotypes, would require a similarly reclusive lifestyle. While the media and others seem to think they have Muslims figured out, the truth is that Americans have little knowledge of true Islam and what Muslims are really like. We in the United States rely on biased media reporting, generalizations, and stories we've heard about Muslims to characterize Islam. But Muslims, especially American Muslims, are the victims of mistaken identity. Our fellow citizens think all Muslims are terrorists and women-oppressors, yet Muslims know we are actually much better people than the stereotypes make us out to be.

In college I would often bring Islam into class discussions. Sometimes I would continue these discussions with professors and fellow students after class. What always surprised me was how much people did not know about Islam. I remember a political science professor sheepishly confessing his ignorance of Islam. We were both a little disheartened by his admission; if he held a doctorate, shouldn't he have a general knowledge of Islam? In addition, if he, as one of the better educated people in the country, didn't think he knew enough about Islam, how many people truly know *nothing* about Islam? The challenge for American Muslims is to educate our fellow non-Muslim citizens about us and to help Americans rise above the misinformation.

Muslims hold prominent positions in American society, as chief executive officers, doctors, partners in law firms, architects, consultants, accountants, investment bankers, writers, journalists, social service workers, and engineers. As they actively build coalitions with each other and with other like-minded groups for various purposes—political influence and gender equality, among others—American Muslims are finally reaching an unprecedented level of recognition.

Some American Muslims are rediscovering their roots. Muslims are realizing how like their own lives was the Prophet's. The Prophet Muhammad's emigration in 622 from Mecca, in Saudi Arabia, to Medina about 250 miles north, was called the *hijra*. The *hijra* was a defining moment for Islam because Muhammad moved from his hometown so that he and his followers could live their religion in freedom away from those against his movement in Mecca. American Muslims see themselves as being in their own small *hijras*. Muhammad's life mirrors some aspects of the plight of Muslims in America: struggling against oppression in varying forms, in search of an authentic identity and freedom of expression. In America, the land of opportunity, the belief in human beings' ability to overcome negative forces is all the more resounding.

Many American Muslims feel strongly that American values and Islamic values, as derived from the Qur'an and *hadith* (traditions and sayings of the Prophet Muhammad are similar—self-respect, an emphasis on family, and the importance of education, of supporting oneself, of contributing to society, and of individualism. In essence, being a Muslim can often mean being an American.

The most significant connection between American society and Islamic values is the idea of self-improvement in an open and free environment. For example, Muhammad himself was a businessman who provided for his family by working hard. In fact, with the emergence of Islam and its emphasis on economic self-sufficiency, the caravan trading routes of Arabia flourished. These Islamic values complement an American lifestyle, and, for that reason, American Muslims believe that they, as Muslims, preserve some of the best aspects of American culture.

What the Muslims of America want today is really no different from what the Mayflower Pilgrims wanted: a better life, a new identity, a society where they can live their beliefs and contribute to the overall good. The only "secret" agenda American Muslims may have is to improve the public image of Muslims.

My hope is that thoughtful Americans are willing to open their minds and learn about Islam, and Islam in America. American Muslims combine the best of Islamic values and culture with America's respect for individualism and an open society. The result is a racially diverse group of people, with roots in the Middle East, Pakistan, Indonesia, and all over the world, who are committed to certain core beliefs and are working to improve the communities in which they live.

In college I represented Muslim students on the college chaplaincy's multi-faith council, which worked with the Dean of Religious Life, Victor Kazanjian, to instill spirituality in the college community. My college had done something quite brave and progressive in eliminating a single-faith chaplaincy in favor of a chaplaincy that represented the religions students on campus actually practiced. Victor often told us that multi-faith was about *moving beyond tolerance* of other faiths to *understanding* other faiths. Though it was difficult for us to open up and talk freely about religion at first, such a dialogue was rewarding. I was fascinated by the stories of other traditions, like the miracle of oil for the candles in the Jewish tradition, remembered during Hanukkah.

One of the stories Victor told us really struck me: In a village with many wells, small groups of people would gather around each well and drink only from that well. Though no one really talked about it, each group thought the water from their own well was the most special. One day, a diver went down through the depths of one of these wells because he wanted to know what was at the bottom. He swam for a very long time because the well was quite deep. When he finally reached the bottom, he found, to his surprise, that all the wells were drawing from the same, large source of water at the bottom of all the wells. By going deep into one well, the diver discovered this.

This story holds a potent theme for all Americans, as today we often are expected to choose a system of beliefs and values to the exclusion of all others. Yet being an American means that when we subscribe to one, we don't have to disregard the others.

Islam and Slavery in Early American History: The *Roots* Story

"So, are you going to talk about Alex Haley in your book?" my mother asked me one day. "Noooo," I said, all smart-alec-y, "Why would I do that?" I couldn't think of what Alex Haley himself, besides writing *The Autobiography of Malcolm X,* had to do with Islam in America. "Should I?" I asked gruffly. I knew that this brainstorm of my mother's was probably going to cause *me* hours, maybe days, of research!

"Well, Alex Haley researched his family tree all the way back to Gambia in Africa. His ancestor, Kunta Kinte, was Muslim and was brought here as a slave."

"Really?" I said, totally surprised.

"Yes! Isn't it interesting? You are too young to remember when the miniseries came out, but Kunta Kinte was a Muslim." From the vaults of my brain, a television scene that I could not place was replayed in my mind's eye. "What is your name?" a man yelled. And, in the camera's close-up, the beaten slave shifted against the wooden post he was chained to and groaned, "Kunta Kinte."

"In the book," my mom said, "Kunta Kinte knows there is a difference between slaves under Islamic law and the American slave he became. Alex Haley writes about it in his book *Roots*. It's very interesting, but I don't know where it is in the book." Hmmmm, I thought to myself. Mom and I looked at each other and realized an idea was coming over us. I had always known *Roots* to be a depiction of slavery and, through the telling of Haley's own family story, of the African-American experience. What if Kunta was Muslim, and there was a discussion of slavery in *Roots?* It would be a totally fresh take on the whole story, now that we know more about Islam in America. Could Kunta Kinte be one of America's first Muslims? Could Muslims have been in America for, well, centuries?

Upon finding a copy of the Bible-sized *Roots,* I realized that this was not going to be an all-nighter-only project. Being a prudent researcher, I put off reading *Roots* until I had asked everyone I knew who had read *Roots* whether they remembered the passage my mom had recalled. When my last resort said she remembered nothing specific, I gave up and gave in. I would just have to read *Roots* myself.

Before I knew it, I was totally absorbed by the story of Kunta Kinte's life in his village, Juffure. From page one, it was clear that Kunta and the members of his village were Muslims. So that mystery was solved. I had nearly forgotten about finding the passage on Islam's view of slavery when I suddenly came across it. Young Kunta Kinte had heard stories of *toubobs,* as they called white men in the Mandinka tongue, stealing Africans away to make "slaves" out of them. Sometimes whole villages of Africans were taken by slave traders and others kidnapped, never to be seen or heard from again. Kunta's younger brother, Lamin, who looked up to Kunta immensely, even asked him one day what a slave was. Not knowing the answer, Kunta ignored Lamin, only later to ask his father, Omoro. His father explained how people became slaves, some born of slave mothers, some becoming slaves to avoid starvation and in exchange for food and shelter, and a third type was taken as a prisoner.

Omoro added that nevertheless slaves were respected as people. "'Their rights are guaranteed by the laws of our forefathers,' said Omoro, and he explained that all masters had to provide their slaves with food, clothing, a house, a farm plot to work on half shares, and also a wife or a husband."[1] He explained how slaves could buy their freedom through what they earned in their farming or win their freedom by marrying into the family that owned them. When Kunta reached manhood, he would sit in on the Council of the Elders' meetings and note how slaves were allowed to bring up disputes against their owner, disputes the Elders carefully analyzed. At other times, slaves came to the Elders with their masters, asking for permission to marry into the owner's family.[2]

Juffure's slaves, which were held according to Qur'anic guide-lines, were treated much better than America's slaves. When Kunta was still young, Omoro told him and Lamin what he and his brothers, hiding in the bushes, had seen of Africans the toubob had taken to their big boats. He tried to make his boys understand the severity with which the toubob dealt with their slaves and how their method was different from how the slaves in their village were treated by their owners. The toubob's slaves were beaten, sometimes burned, their heads shaved, bodies greased, teeth, throats and private parts examined, and they were chained to each other. "'You cannot be told these things strongly enough,' said their father. 'You must know what your uncles and I saw happening to those who had been stolen. It is the difference between slaves among ourselves and those whom the toubob takes away to be slaves for him.'"[3] He implored them never to go anywhere outside the village alone if they could possibly help it.

Yet Kunta did go outside his village alone one day, not very far, to chop wood, with which he was going to make a drum. He was about sixteen years old. Before he knew it, he was kidnapped and gone from his village forever. The image of Kunta, stolen from his village and the whole life he knew, is burned into my mind. Haley, in his research, verified as fact that his ancestor Kunta Kinte had been chopping wood when he was taken. The story of young Kunta had been passed down orally through generations of Haley's family. Imagine Haley's stunned astonishment when an African *griot,* a record-keeper who passes down stories to the next generation of *griots*, who knew the history of the Kinte family, repeated the same story of young Kunta's disappearance while chopping wood for a drum.

I have to say that Haley's book is bittersweet for me. I kept hoping beyond hope that Kunta would somehow return to Africa and be reunited with the mother he loved and the younger brothers he adored and the father whom he looked up to. Some African Muslims did actually return to Africa, but very few.[4] There are no Hollywood-scripted reunions to Kunta's story. In fact, Kunta's new American family was ripped apart again in America. I shared in Haley's joy as he uncovered his roots, but I soon remembered that slavery caused the separation of Haley from his roots. Should we rejoice that Haley found his family, when he and his ancestors didn't have to be separated in the first place?

Depending on your view of history, Islam in America can be categorized as an old phenomenon. Muslims may have been in America as far back as 800 years ago! *When did Muslims first arrive in America?* It may seem a silly question to ask. We all know that today's Muslims either immigrated here or are indigenous converts to Islam. However, this question becomes more important as American Muslims search for an American identity. In that search, many are surprised to learn of evidence that suggests that Muslims sailed to and explored North America in 1178, maybe even earlier—and yes, that is before Columbus. In addition, strong evidence shows that a Moroccan Muslim named Estevanico or Estephan is believed to have arrived in Florida in 1539 as part of a Spanish expedition that would take him to Arizona and New Mexico, making him one of the first men to cross North America.[5]

The most astonishing fact about Islam in early American history is that the first major immigration of Muslims to America was, actually, through the slave trade as described in *Roots!* Slaves who professed belief in Allah and Muhammad and didn't eat pork, presumably Muslims, arrived in North America in 1717 and throughout the slavery period from 1619 to 1863.[6] Most American slaves were brought from Africa's West Coast, particularly from Islamic countries such as present-day Ghana, the Ivory Coast, Burkina Faso, Niger, and Algeria. Of the over ten million Africans brought to America as slaves, 20 to 30 percent or more were Muslim like Kunta Kinte.[7] Many journalists and scholars agree that at least one-fifth of African slaves brought to America were Muslim, with most eventually converting to Christianity.[8] The number of Muslim-African slaves may be higher, as 62 percent of Africa is Muslim today.[9]

In references to the book since its publication, a much over-looked aspect of Alex Haley's book *Roots* is Haley's Muslim ancestry, an oversight that is reflective of the ignorance regarding the religion of African slaves. We know that Africans were thought of as naked savages wielding spears, running amok in dark jungles. Because it tells a story that exemplifies the slave experience in America through generations, reading *Roots* is like unlocking and sifting through the contents of a gigantic treasure chest. Besides Haley's *Roots* and a few other books, there are too few efforts to uncover the strong family structures, value systems, intellectual achievements, and great pride of African people. Many of those who do try to connect a great culture and history with the peoples of Africa use inadequate research or are written off and negatively labeled as "Afro-Centrists" in the academic community.

Kunta Kinte, Haley's great-great-great-great-grandfather, was a Muslim before he was a slave, kidnapped by slave traders while chopping wood near his village to make a drum. He prayed to Allah five times a day as did all the other men in Juffure, his village, and he followed other guidelines of Islam. He had grown up in Juffure and lived there sixteen years before he was kidnapped, his growth into manhood, greater respect, and responsibility in Juffure cut off abruptly. He landed in Annapolis, Maryland, on September 29, 1767. Why, and how, was Kunta Muslim?

Islam had spread to Africa over time and possibly during the Prophet Muhammad's lifetime. Muhammad himself knew several Africans and may have been of African descent himself, as his own antecedent Prophet Ismail's (Ishmael) mother may have been African. In addition, Muhammad is said to have been raised by a black Abyssinian woman, whose African husband, Zaid, was a companion of the Prophet's. Another companion of Muhammad's, Bilal, is famous among Muslims as being a freed slave who gave the first ever *adhan,* or call to prayer, in the history of Islam. Historical accounts say that Bilal had a melodious voice and was directed by the Prophet, both for his voice and his devoutness, to make the *adhan*. Besides Bilal, the black Moors of Spain and

Portugal and the African Muslims made a great contribution to the spread of the Islamic empire.

Because of his exposure to Africans, Muhammad made a point of talking about race and racial differences. In his last sermon at Mecca, on his last pilgrimage, Muhammad told the group of Muslims gathered before him that the superior among them were those who feared the Lord, not those of a particular race.[10] The Qur'an in fact specifies that God divided the people of the world into tribes and nations not so that we should try to dominate each other or become racists but so that we can *know* and learn of each other in an organized and efficient manner.

The late Fazlur Rahman, a pre-eminent American Muslim scholar on Islam and a gifted writer, in his book *Major Themes of the Qur'an* compared slavery in Islam to the practice of polygamy, saying of polygamy that, "The truth seems to be that permission for polygamy was at a legal plane while the sanctions put on it were in the nature of a *moral ideal towards which the society was expected to move,* since it was not possible to remove polygamy legally at one stroke. We encounter a similar phenomenon with regard to slavery." He goes on to say that in the Qur'an, while slavery is accepted, emancipation of slaves is highly encouraged (see Qur'anic verses 90:13; 5:89; 58:3; 24:33). In fact, the Qur'an instructed Muslims to allow their slaves to buy their freedom through payment of an agreed-upon sum.[11] Though such action was only recommended, others feel strongly that Islam is actually strongly against slavery.[12] Those of us who believe in the progressiveness of Islam can call Muhammad an emancipator and the Qur'an an emancipation proclamation. At the very least, Islam espoused a progressiveness on slavery that was rare at that time.

In addition, the Qur'an specifies that Muslims should treat their slaves well. For example, certain needs must be met, such as providing shelter and food as well as fulfilling requests for a spouse, as described in *Roots.* In addition, if a child was born of an unmarried slave woman, her master must treat that child as if it were his own. As a result, those children received their share of the father's inheritance just like his other children.

Some ruling Islamic families even passed down their leadership to their children born of slaves, resulting in slave dynasties in some parts of the Islamic world. Obviously a big difference exists between the treatment of slaves as prescribed by the Qur'an and the treatment of slaves throughout the world.

We all know the end of Alex Haley's story. So we know that Kunta never goes back to Africa. Though unable to return to his African family, Kunta begins a new family in the United States. Tragically, Kunta's daughter is sold and eventually bears her owner's child. Even though Kunta never met his own grandson or saw his mother again, Haley through fortuitous research patches together his family tree, in essence preserving his family forever. So while I still ache at the thought of Kunta's capture, I realize that I'm glad Alex Haley is an American, because who else would have written *Roots* and *The Autobiography of Malcolm X,* enriching the lives of Americans and people around the world? I do not mean to justify slavery; who can justify the unjustifiable? What I mean to say is that something good, *Roots,* and the way *Roots* has changed the way people think of Africans and African-Americans and slavery, is a positive social outcome. We—meaning America, the West, those who participated in the slave trade—destroyed the family structure Africans had built over centuries when Africans were brought to America as slaves. We separated mothers from children, husbands from wives. Now, people like my mom see the destruction of the family unit as the legacy of slavery, not as the side-effect of welfare, or the remnant of a stereotypically savage African culture.

As I was reading *Roots,* I was giving my parents, especially my mom, a play-by-play of the plot. I was on vacation, which had taken me from the Cayman Islands to Europe, and I was sitting at high tea with my mom in London's Lanesborough

Hotel recounting the sale of Kunta and his wife's beloved daughter Kizzy and how horrifying it was. By the time I finished *Roots* we were back home in Pueblo, Colorado. Though exhausted from jetlag I stayed awake until three in the morning finishing the last pages of *Roots* in which Haley describes how he was able to track his family back to Kunta Kinte and the village based on a few terse family stories passed down orally.

My parents and I talked about *Roots* at dinner the next night. For once, I was able to speak without my parents' interrupting, as they sat in rapt attention while I described Haley's research. When I finished, my dad looked at my mom and said, "How sad. It really was a holocaust."

"You know, it reminds me of the Alhambra," my mom said. "I know it sounds silly, but I felt the spirits of the Muslims there. It was . . . " she paused, looking for the right word, " . . . haunting." She and my father talked about the Alhambra and the slave trade for a while. My mom blurted out, toward the end of the conversation, "That's why it's hard for many Muslims to trust Europeans!"

"Huh?" I said to go with my dad's "Hmm?" We had no idea what mom meant. "Every time Muslims have met Europeans," she began, "bad things have happened eventually. Why should Muslims trust Europeans?" I tried to put a positive spin on things, reasoning that the Alhambra is now a treasure open to the world. If it were still held by Muslims, maybe the world wouldn't have a chance to see it at all. But I couldn't really come up with a positive spin for slavery. And mom wouldn't have been pleased with it anyway, as she wasn't pleased with the Alhambra apology. But we really should be aware of the spirits that haunt us. Recognizing history and feeling it in its most raw and pure form is how we will learn.

Today's African-Americans are irrevocably cut from their African customs and lives and, for some, their Muslim heritage. When African-Americans convert to Islam, though, they are actually, possibly, returning to their own roots, in a sense "reverting" to Islam. Today, with a sizable American Muslim population, we can see *Roots* from the perspective of the American Muslim journey—

from isolation, alienation, and small numbers to greater recognition and a viable community within the American community. We can feel African-American conversion as a victory, in a sense, for humankind, a reclaiming of identity and pride, a becoming comfortable with our spirits.

CLOSE-UP
The Sects of Islam

When I started boarding school in eighth grade, I was surprised to find out that there was another Muslim student, a sophomore, at the school, in addition to me and my sister. (This was before two Muslims would join my class the next year.) I still had not met many Muslims outside my own family. My sister told my mom about this other Muslim student on Parents' Weekend that year and added tentatively, "But she's a different kind of Muslim, mom. She's like 'she'-something."

"Shi'ite," my mom corrected. "They are another branch of Islam." I'm sure my sister and I said in response, "Huh?" Then mom explained to us that Islam has sects, as Christianity does. "Your classmate and her family are Shi'ite Muslims, and we are Sunni Muslims, just as there are Baptist Christians and Catholic Christians."

My mom didn't go into specifics, but later I learned that the two major sects of Islam are Sunnism and Shi'ism, with the overwhelming majority of world and American Muslims being Sunni. In addition, a few other sects, the largest of which is the Ismaili Muslims, also exist. Estimates place Shi'ite Muslims, those who follow the other major sect of Islam, at 10 to 16 percent of the American Muslim population. Shi'ites account for about 10 percent of the world Muslim population as well, thus making the Sunni-Shi'ite distribution in America proportional to the world Sunni-Shi'ite distribution, which is about 84 to 90 percent Sunni and 10 to 16 percent Shia.[1]

The sectional divisions seem arbitrary at first, because Sunnis and Shias do not disagree on the major tenets of Islam. All Muslims follow the Five Pillars of Islam, believe in the Qur'an, and follow the teachings of the Prophet Muhammad. In addition to these and many other similarities in worship, most Muslims are Sunni anyway. So why bother emphasizing a difference that seems inconsequential?

However, the distinctions are important because they determine who a Muslim looks to as a leader. Sunni Muslims follow
the teachings of the Qur'an and Prophet Muhammad only.
Shi'ite Muslims, on the other hand, also follow the sayings and
traditions of Muhammad's son-in-law, Ali. The Shia sect actually
derives its origins from a group of Muslims who supported Ali
against his political enemies, and the emphasis stuck. Shias truly
believe that Ali is a very important person in Islam. To some, he is
as important as the Prophet himself, maybe more. In addition,
Iran and Iraq are majority Shi'ite countries while the rest of the
Islamic world is mostly Sunni.[2] A different minority Muslim community in South Asia follow the teachings of Mirza Ghulam
Ahmad. For that reason, they are called "Ahmadis" or "Marzais."
They have been persecuted in Pakistan for blasphemy and therefore have spread out all over the world.

The Muslims of the Ismaili sect, though small in number, are
significant in that they believe Allah has a representative on
Earth, working on his behalf, called the Aga Khan. Ismaili
Muslims also believe that the Aga Khan is a descendant of
Prophet Muhammad, and that his job is to interpret the Qur'an
for Ismaili Muslims. This position is actually a hereditary one,
as the title of "Aga Khan" has been passed down through one
family for centuries. The Aga Khan is famous among non-
Muslims for a few reasons. First, he is quite wealthy, due to
"dues" Ismaili Muslims must pay him. Second, though he does
maintain a lavish lifestyle with homes in Europe and so forth,
the Aga Khan funds all sorts of humanitarian and charitable
causes throughout the world. He is a world-class philanthropist,
up there with some of the world's richest men, like Ted Turner
and George Soros, establishing free hospitals for the poor in
third-world countries and donating funds to libraries specifically
earmarked for purchasing books on Islam. Third, many have
heard of the Aga Khan because in the 1950's the son of the then
Aga Khan (Aly Khan) married Hollywood actress Rita Hayworth,
shocking world Muslims and Americans alike.

Some say that the Aga Khan's days are numbered, that followers are tired of paying him portions of their income for little

religious guidance in return. In addition, some non-Ismaili Muslims criticize Ismaili Muslims for being lax in following some of Islam's guidelines, such as no drinking of alcohol. An Ismaili Muslim I know calls Ismailis a "lost sect." Furthermore, many Muslims are quick to point out that the idea of Allah's having a representative on Earth is un-Islamic since Muslims believe that Muhammad was Allah's last prophet. Some would also say that Ismaili Muslims, at about one percent of the world's total Muslim population, are too small a group to sustain themselves. However, we must remember that one percent of 1.2 billion is still a lot of people!

I have to admit I have a small fascination with the Aga Khan, mostly because in college I was able to find a number of books on Islam that I otherwise couldn't have found in the Massachusetts Institute of Technology (MIT) library, to which the Aga Khan had given money to buy books on Islam. The position of Aga Khan is the last vestige of a much older tradition, yet the current Aga Khan seems modern. I met him once briefly, and he is charismatic. Imagine a more hip Pope John Paul II (though having fewer followers and less divine authority), wearing a European business suit. He is becoming older, and rumors have it that he would like to pass on his title to his daughter over his sons though such an unprecedented move could be disastrous for the community, maybe even the death knell if Ismaili men refuse to serve a female Aga Khan.

But I've noticed a revitalization of the Ismaili sect in America. American Ismaili Muslims are active, raising money for many causes. Furthermore, I have a feeling that if the Aga Khan does appoint his daughter, Muslims like me will rally around his decision. I think it's about time a prominent Muslim acknowledge the contributions of women as the Prophet did. So I would say to the Aga Khan and his daughter: "You go girl and father!"

Though American Sunni, Shi'ite, and Ismaili communities sometimes separate for worship, they do not have tense relations. Like the majority of Muslims, I am Sunni. But living in America, where most people are Christian, being a Sunni Muslim is not as important or as noticed as simply being Muslim. Would I marry a Shi'ite or an Ismaili? Would my family let me? I don't really know. (At this point, my family has the attitude: marry whomever, just marry before you become an old hag!) Joking aside, the communities do have anxieties about each other that are manifested when intermarriage occurs. Shi'ites are seen, by both Sunnis and others, as more extreme than Sunni Muslims. Some Shi'ite rituals are very dramatic, including one in which Shi'ites beat their breasts in atonement for a centuries-old battle in which Shi'ites attacked Sunnis. I would say that nowadays you won't see a Shi'ite beating himself or herself black and blue for this, but it does show how on some issues, Shi'ites feel more strongly than Sunnis do.

In America today, I would say it is no longer religious sects that are a source of division for American Muslims, but their ethnic diversity. Their various ethnicities—whether Palestinian or Pakistani or African-American—prevent American Muslims from having a single opinion on practically any issue at a time when unity is necessary to wield political influence in America. American Muslims don't emphasize our sects because we have so much else to emphasize: our status as a religious minority in America and our ethnic divisions.

—— *2* ◆ The American Muslim ————

So who are these American Muslims? And what do they want? I often heard variations on those two questions when I told people I was writing this book. When I think of my religion, I don't instantly think of the roughly six to nine million Muslims living with me in the United States—including other children of immigrants who are working for investment banks, or the numerous Pakistani cab drivers, or the prisoners who have converted to Islam.[1] But that is my community, a large and diverse one.

For example, let's say we're looking at one block in New York City. In one building is an office for a major consulting firm, and the consultants there are busy at work. In an office in the same building, the owner of a travel agency is thinking about hiring more agents, as his business is rapidly growing. Next door is a three-star hotel, and the manager is frantically working the front desk trying to process all the check-ins and check-outs. In one of the rooms, a concert promoter is touching base with the band members he's currently working with. On the same block, a CEO is in a 7–11 store, asking the man behind the counter if they have a particular brand of toothpaste. It is entirely possible that all the people I've described are Muslim. In fact, I personally know Muslims who fit the above profiles. Are you surprised? I guess, to some degree, I'm even a little surprised myself. But if you think about the people you know, I'm sure you've met at least one Muslim. Between you, your family, and your friends, you probably know a lot more Muslims than you realize, with more varied occupations and backgrounds than you think. American Muslims are found in all walks of life from sea to shining sea.

As for what American Muslims want, to tell the truth, they don't all want one specific political goal like electing a Muslim president or a specific social goal such as opening a mosque in every American town. We're too diverse to have one issue to rally around. For example, if all American Muslims were African-American only, they would probably focus on domestic policy and specifically issues that affect the African-American community. Though African-Americans are the largest American Muslim group, about 42 percent of the American Muslim population, they are not the entire community. South Asian Muslims are the next largest group at about 24 percent and then Arab Muslims at about 12 percent. Beyond those three major groups, people of other ethnicities also make up the American Muslim population, including white Americans, Africans, Southeast Asians, and so on. In that sense, American Muslims prove the Islamic principle of racial equality. In Islam, no race or country is favored over other races and countries. You can see from the ethnic and national diversity of American Muslims that we come from all over the globe.

Our greatest challenge is overcoming our public image as terrorists, followed closely by the need to unify, despite our different ethnicities, so that we can contribute in a significant and positive way to American society and take our place alongside other groups as a part of American culture.

That may sound scary to you: six million plus people unifying! I would be scared too, especially if I thought all these people were terrorists. I would probably write to my representative in Congress and request some action against these bad people. I would also be wary of anything they do to try to make themselves look better because I would wonder if this move was a part of their grand scheme to take over the world.

That's why I'm writing this book: simply to say that American Muslims don't pose a threat to the United States or to the world. In many ways, the United States will benefit from American Muslims' attempts to strengthen their own community. For example, as Muslims unify beyond ethnicities and nationalities and create organizations in which they all work together, their experience can be a model for all Americans. In essence, Muslims' struggle to come together mirrors, or is a microcosm of, the struggle of all Americans to come together.

American Muslims must gain a better public image. When, for example, Mrs. Ida Smith, out in Idaho, hears of Muslims, she thinks of the World Trade Center bombing, the hostage crisis with Iran, the protests against *The Satanic Verses,* and she probably imagines that Muslims are downright un-American. Admittedly, if that was all I knew about Muslims, I would think they pose a threat to our way of life, too.

Knowing that Americans have the wrong idea frustrates American Muslims. I remember walking back to my dorm one spring day of my junior year in college and running into my good friend Lara, who had incredibly bad news. "This federal building in Oklahoma City was bombed, and they don't think there are any survivors!" she said.

"What?" I asked in shock. Like others, I first reacted to the news of death and destruction with disbelief. Lara repeated what she said and added that officials did not know, as yet, who was behind the bombing. As I internalized the seriousness of the situation, my immediate thought was, "I hope a Muslim didn't do it." Before any evidence pointing to a suspect became available, so-called experts were all over American television saying that this was the act of a Muslim terrorist and characteristic of Arab terrorism. The suited torsos and coifed hairdos of men like Steve Emerson, who were proven wrong with Timothy McVeigh's arrest and later conviction, were projected into our cozy living rooms, as they spewed tales of the characteristics of a Middle Eastern bombing fitting the Oklahoma bombing.

Between the time of the Oklahoma City bombing and the arrest of McVeigh for that bombing, there were a few moments when I had to ask myself, "Is this really happening?" I also asked myself, "I'm in the United States of America, aren't I?" What was I supposed to think when all I heard on radio and television and read in the newspapers was major anti-Islamic sentiment? During the days before McVeigh was arrested, I felt as though I was in an intellectual coma—I was the first to admit that Muslim terrorists are responsible for bad things, but I wasn't ready to condemn all of Islamic civilization merely for being Muslim.

The stereotypes that media reports spawned—that every Arab or dark, foreign-looking, bearded man or every woman in headcover is a terrorist—have consequences. How much time did federal agents lose in finding the real perpetrators while chasing bearded men? One Muslim man was detained at an airport for hours on the basis of his religion and the fact that he had ties to Oklahoma City. Muslims were treated poorly in their communities, particularly the Muslims of Oklahoma. As an American, I wanted the perpetrators caught. Additionally as an American, I didn't want to get caught up in grandiose talk of ancient hatreds, warlike ways, and tendencies for destruction that didn't find the perpetrators or lessen the suffering of the victims and their families.

With the Oklahoma City bombing, American Muslims came to the edge of a cliff and began looking over, and the bottom of that cliff is the treatment of Japanese-Americans during World War II, when they were held in internment camps, denied their rights as American citizens, and singled out as un-American. You may think I'm being dramatic, but let's analyze this situation.

My own congressman at the time, a *close* family friend who had spent much time with us, made venomous statements against the Middle East after hearing about the bombing. His statements were printed in the local newspapers.

Soon after, we received a threatening letter, directed against my family as foreigners and Muslim. This happened despite the fact that we had lived in Pueblo for twenty years and had many friends there.

The media frenzy against Muslims was so strong that the only question was which Islamic group was responsible—one from Iran, Iraq, or even from the United States.

What if a Muslim had done it? Islam would be confirmed as undemocratic and anti-Western. If our congressman, a family friend, could rely on stereotypes and condemn Islam (though he later apologized sincerely when my mother reproached him), how can I expect the average American to learn to distinguish between me and a terrorist, and also to realize there are a lot more Muslims like me and not like the terrorists? Even if a Muslim had been behind the blast, we, as Americans, should be smart enough and understanding enough to realize that not all Muslims would commit such acts. In fact, the vast majority never would.

American Muslims and world Muslims can't be wholly described by the "Muslim McVeighs" of their world. This has always been a problem for Islam and American Muslims: why can't non-Muslims understand that one Muslim does not represent all of us? There's always a rush to lump all Muslims together, to interpret Islam as a belligerent faith, and to characterize Muslim women as universally oppressed. Not to shock anyone, but the truth is: not all Muslims are alike, Islam advocates peace and understanding over war, and Muslim women enjoy certain rights as specified in the Qur'an. If you are a sensible person, you must ask yourself, why would a billion plus people including six million Americans subscribe to a religion that is homogenous, belligerent, and oppressive to women? That would make no sense! How could that many people subscribe to such backward philosophies? The truth is: they don't. Unfortunately, we have not asked ourselves such questions, and we continue to believe in stereotypes and misunderstandings. In fact, Islam may be the topic Americans know the least about, and misunderstand the most.

Misunderstanding of Islam and the spreading of stereotypes about Muslims are as prevalent in U.S. society as the discrimination against overweight people and smokers. Americans realize these injustices occur on a subconscious level and rarely do anything about them. I don't think Americans have intentionally declared that they do not want to know more about Islam. I do not think Americans enjoy using stereotypes and generalizations. I think they just haven't realized yet how much they don't know about Muslims.

It's an uphill battle, but to American Muslims' credit, the hard work in improving our image has resulted in an improvement of the media's treatment of Islam. Oklahoma made the media take a deep breath and realize they had committed a grand rush to judgment. Now Muslims are not always the first to be accused by media commentators, but those commentators still have lapses in judgment and accuracy.

I know I still live in fear of anti-Muslim hysteria. Every time a bombing is suspected, on an airplane, as with TWA Flight 800, or in public places, like the Atlanta Centennial Olympic Park bombing, I, like probably all American Muslims, say to myself, "I hope a Muslim didn't do it." This thought almost precludes my sadness for the victims. It is so much easier to blame a large, ambiguous group of people who have always been seen as foreign, the "other," and so unlike us Americans, than to think of the Muslim you know personally who lives down the street or who runs the Indian restaurant you like. As a Muslim, I am very comfortable being American. I just wonder when, as a society, we'll know that Muslims are Americans too, just as there are Catholics who are Americans, Chinese people who are Americans, and so on. I don't think that's a lot to ask. I believe in Americans' ability to learn and to improve our society.

The next step for American Islam is a major give-and-take between Muslim Americans and non-Muslim Americans, genuine on both sides: American Muslims must not be ashamed to educate, and non-Muslims must not be ashamed to learn. It sounds easy, but I think it's hard for one person to say to another, "Can I ask you some questions about your religion?" It's also easy to become frustrated if one is trying to explain something and one's listener continues to resort to stereotypes.

I remember once in college my roommate, Alexandra, dragged me to a showing of final projects from the video production class. One was a series of interviews of various people, edited together. I knew one woman because she was in my gay literature class, and I presumed she was a lesbian, though I didn't really bother to ask because I didn't think it was my business.

I was a little intimidated by this woman and others in the class because they seemed to project a coolness I couldn't comprehend. I was quite convinced I was the only straight woman in the class. At that, I wasn't even a highly experienced straight woman! So there I was, probably the only straight woman in a class of lesbians and bisexual women, and I myself had the least amount of practical knowledge about sex! This class would make even the most unassuming person self-conscious.

So, in this film, about midway through it, the woman in my class said: "I really don't know what it's like to be a Muslim woman, to be a woman in that culture." This shocked me! I had no idea she was curious about being a Muslim woman. I then felt a little embarrassed because, even if she had dozed through most of our gay literature classes, she should have an idea I was Muslim since I was constantly using American Muslims in examples and arguments. Why hadn't she asked me this question?

The film ended, and I saw that the woman was sitting in the row in front of me. I walked down my row and sat down in a seat behind her and tapped her on the shoulder. She turned to see who was tapping her, and, with her scarf and dark glasses, she evoked for a moment the glamour of fifties' movie stars.

"Hi!" I said, "I just wanted to tell you that I am a Muslim woman, and I would be happy to talk to you at any time about being Muslim and female."

"Oh," she said nervously. Then she just giggled, almost out of embarrassment. She didn't say anything, so I added something like, "Well, give me a call, if you want," and left.

I never heard from that woman, ever. I was surprised, too. At Wellesley, we were constantly encouraged to share with one another, and I was certainly ready to share and learn. Yet, this woman wasn't. I have no idea why she didn't call me, and why we didn't chat about things. It wouldn't have been easy for me either, but I thought it would be useful for both of us to talk about something she had questions about, and I had some answers for. I was hurt, too. I thought I had made an effort to listen to others in our class, but this woman couldn't do that for me.

I eventually told my mother how disappointed I was that this woman and I hadn't ever spoken. I told my mom that I felt as though she had played on people's stereotypes of Muslim women for shock value, to make herself look inquisitive, sensitive, and intelligent. But when push came to shove, she really *didn't* want to know what it was like to be a Muslim woman. Her comment was just superficial.

"No!" my mother replied excitedly. (For a second I thought my mom was going to say that this woman must have had a crush on me and was too embarassed to talk to me.) "Asma, if this woman said that, it means she must have thought about it a little bit first." My mom persuaded me that somewhere in this woman's brain curiosity on the subject of Islam had registered, and that was a good start. "If a lesbian, somebody outside of mainstream society, is curious about Muslims," my mom said, "then everybody else must be too." I liked my mom's more optimistic and mature view of this woman: I want to believe that Americans and others are interested in Muslims beyond mere shock value.

CLOSE-UP
Hijab and the Single Girl: Will Men Ever Learn to Control Themselves?

Hijab, or the head cover many Muslim women wear, is probably the most enigmatic aspect of Islam in America, for both
Americans and American Muslims. Alexander McQueen, British
fashion designer for Givenchy and a non-Muslim, created a "couture chador, inspired by a photograph from *National Geographic*."
According to a story in *Vogue* (October 1997), he added his own
innovation by attaching a cage holding a live bird to the top of the
hijab. For Americans, the *hijab* looks repressive and may serve as
symbolic proof of the stereotype that Muslim women are
oppressed. For American Muslims, the *hijab* represents the eye of
the storm, with the storm being how American Muslims are interpreting the Qur'an and bringing their modern perspectives to it.
To some, wearing *hijab* is a way of showing physically a preservation of traditional Islam, as it was practiced in the country from
which the immigrants came, or to show that they are serious
about being Muslim. I have no doubt that conservative Muslims'
hearts are elated when they see a young woman wearing *hijab*, as
if that proves that Islam is surviving in the United States. To others, wearing *hijab* is an act of devotion, a way of serving God.

So where did *hijab* come from? Though there are accounts of
head-covering in pre-Islamic Arabia (which would explain why
Catholic nuns wear, in essence, *hijab,* not to mention that it is
shown in practically every representation of the Virgin Mary),
the Islamic basis for *hijab* is a few Qur'anic passages. The first
asks that men and women be modest in their appearance and
lower their gaze when with the opposite sex. The majority of
world Muslims have come to interpret this to mean that women
should cover their heads when out in public. The second passage
instructs that men and women should cover their heads while
praying. Some Muslims read this and come to the conclusion that
since everything they do in life is a prayer and/or in service to
God they should always cover their heads.

I have a few problems with seeing *hijab* as a Qur'anic requirement, the main one being that, if the above interpretations are true, men are severely, disproportionately, excluded from the *hijab* requirement, particularly in the United States. The modesty passage is directed to both men and women as is the prayer passage. In addition, the modesty passage does not necessarily suggest covering one's head. It actually specifies arms and chest. Furthermore, if everything we do is an expression of prayer, men as well as women should be required to wear *hijab* as there is no exception in the Qur'an. (It does not say "Only womens' actions count as prayer.") Finally, if the whole point of wearing *hijab* is *not to attract attention* to oneself, *hijab* in America certainly does not serve that purpose. Instead it epitomizes the phrase "sticking out like a sore thumb."

The disproportionate application of *hijab* bothers me. I would truly care less about the issue of *hijab* if men wore something similar. I shared this thought with my brother while I was having one of my intellectual rages. "Ali," I said (my family calls my brother by his middle name and not his first name out of respect for the Prophet), "it wouldn't bother me so much that women are going to all this trouble, if men had to do it too." We thought for a moment and realized that Saudi Arabian men cover their heads a la Lawrence of Arabia, an interesting fact considering that Saudia Arabian women are required to cover from head *to toe,* based on Saudi Arabian interpretation of the above Qur'anic passages. My brother and I talked about the matter, and then Ali said, "The Saudi Arabian men must have finally said to the women: 'Fine! We'll wear it too! Now quit complaining!'" Of course, I have no clue why Saudi Arabian men began to cover their heads, but I thought Ali's description was pretty funny.

As you may have gleaned, I don't think the Qur'an and God are asking me to wear *hijab.* I could be wrong, but I believe modesty comes from the inside-out, not the outside-in. I could cover my head but still flirt with my eyes or wear tight clothing. Some young women only wear *hijab* at Islamic gatherings and do not really believe in it. A peer pressure exists at these events. If you looked around and realized you were the only female in the room not wearing a head cover, you would probably feel a little odd. I have experienced that feeling. Usually, when I've noticed it, I've been at an academic Islamic conference, and the women wearing *hijab* there were dressed modestly as well. I attended a much larger, more social gathering of American Muslims and, though I noticed that my sister and I seemed to be the only women not wearing *hijab,* many of the younger women were wearing *hijab* as well as tight pants and blouses, showing off their figures. The hypocrisy stuns me, and I wonder why their parents don't say anything to them. Many women, including the tight-clothing ones, take off their *hijabs* the moment they step outside of such conferences.

This is clearly a contentious issue for American Muslims. It refers directly to the question: how Americanized have Muslims become? A small number of Muslims feel that not wearing *hijab* is tantamount to dating and engaging in premarital sex, a big taboo in American Islam. I don't think my not wearing *hijab* (except when I pray, of course) shows that Islam is losing a battle with American culture, however. What it does show is that being a Muslim in America, and not in an Islamic country with widely held interpretations that are never questioned, has caused me to read the Qur'an myself and find out what it says and how I interpret it. Even if I don't end up toeing the traditional Islamic line and wearing *hijab,* it's great that I have made an effort to read the Qur'an. Had I grown up in Saudi Arabia, I probably would never have bothered to see what the Qur'an really has to say about *hijab* or anything else.

So are women who wear *hijab* no better off than the caged bird of designer Alexander McQueen's couture concoction? In fairness to women who do wear *hijab,* I must point out the many good reasons for it. The greatest advantage may be that, when wearing *hijab,* one is probably not the object of a man's leery glances or intrusive flirtations. You can go out in public and not be bothered. Women who wear *hijab* regularly cite that point and more intellectual reasons as well. They say that you can't appreciate the benefits of *hijab* until you have worn it regularly, that *hijab* liberates a woman from the constricting mores governing appearance such as fashion trends and the societal expectations of how a woman should look. Women who advocate wearing *hijab* say it is liberating in a sense that Western, *Ms.* and NOW-type feminists will never understand.

Though I have never worn *hijab* other than for prayer, I am willing to wager that the disadvantages may outweigh the advantages, mainly due to non-Muslim Americans' treatment of women who wear *hijab*. These women face discrimination both on the job and outside of work. Muslim Rose Hamid of Charlotte, North Carolina, lost her job with U.S. Airways because her scarf apparently violated company uniform rules. She says that since she began wearing *hijab,* she has felt "like a foreigner fighting for . . . acceptance" though she grew up in America. According to the Council on American-Islamic Relations, women call them practically every day with similar complaints of being suspended or fired from work because of their wearing *hijab*.[1] In Aminah Beverly McCloud's essay "African-American Muslim Women," she describes four models of African-American women's conversion experiences. For two of the models, the woman is eventually forced out of her job because of her co-workers' and employer's inability to deal with the changes in her life, *especially* the covering of her hair. Aminah McCloud makes another interesting criticism in her book *African-American Islam:* "The secular nature of American society is often used to force Muslim women out of positions of high visibility."[2] McCloud then asserts that the American environment is based on a diverse secularism and not a tolerance of individuals, making life in America very difficult for a Muslim woman who wears Islamic dress and eats *halal* food.

A respondent to a survey conducted by Carol Anway writes, "One often feels like a fish swimming upstream in America . . . constantly explaining *hijab*. I have been denied jobs because of my *hijab* and . . . otherwise openly discriminated against."[3] Muslim schoolgirls can be teased for their appearance when they wear *hijab* and loose clothing.[4] Wearing Islamic dress has resulted in some Muslim women being ticketed under old state laws against wearing a disguise in public. Paradoxically, such anti-disguise laws were enacted so that law enforcement officials could pursue Ku Klux Klan members, a group whose agenda is completely *different* from that of American Muslim women who simply want to have a modest appearance.[5] Increasingly, more and more women seek redress from their employers for dismissal due to *hijab*.[6] However, most women probably do not. Women who wear *hijab* are spat on, shortchanged (because cashiers think these women can't count) among other indignities. Though Americans are used to Jewish men in yarmulkes and Roman Catholic nuns in habits, they have yet to extend the same courtesy to women wearing *hijab*.[7] As a result of these difficulties, many Muslim women only cover themselves for Islamic functions.[8]

But *hijab* represents a special status to some of the American Muslim women who wear it. The government usually intervenes in cases of religious discrimination, and the suffering inflicted upon Muslim women as a result of wearing *hijab* is counteracted by the empowerment they feel.[9] Medical doctor Zehra Panjvani, who wears *hijab*, spoke at the Islamic Council of New England Conference on "Women in Islam." She said that she is respected by her students and peers, having won three awards for her teaching, but if *hijab* became a barrier to her employment, "If they don't want to hire me [because of *hijab*], I don't want to work for them because they're narrow-minded bigots! Allah will provide a job for me." She continues, "Your character, perhaps, comes out more strongly [in wearing *hijab*]. Your inner self is . . . strong, and that is seen."[10] A number of women express the respect and exhilaration they experience for standing up for their Islamic beliefs.[11]

Is *hijab* a representation of the cultural debate between Americans and American Muslims?[12]

*Hijab*s range in shape and size; they can be tight or loose. You can buy them and other modest Islamic clothing over the internet from CaravanXpress. The question some are asking is, does the Qur'an ask women to cover their heads literally, or is the Qur'an merely asking for women to be modest in appearance? Conservative Muslims do not think there is a question here; the

Qur'an says women must cover their heads. Muslims who are less strict interpreters say that the Qur'anic passages discussing women's modesty are open to a number of interpretations. In response to this view, some Muslims say that *hijab* has been a part of Islamic law for centuries, and American Muslims should not give in to the influence of America's free-spirited culture. Modernists take a practical approach, saying that if *hijab* was so important, the Prophet and the Qur'an would have been "crystal clear" on the issue, which they are not. They feel the culture of various Islamic countries is sinking into theology.[13] In Muhammad's time, only his wives wore *hijab,* and, after his death, upper-class women wore *hijab.*[14]

The result of this debate has been a categorization of where women stand on interpreting the Qur'an by whether they wear *hijab* or not. One California Muslim leader told Robert Marquand of the *Christian Science Monitor:* "Establishment Muslims have made the *hijab* a . . . litmus test for a woman's credentials. . . . The issue is out of control." Marquand reports that women who were not wearing *hijab* were "booed when they tried to speak" at an Islamic conference.[15] The Islamic Council of New England's (ICNE) Conference on "Women in Islam" was notable for several reasons: they had several strong female speakers, and a large number of men attended and listened to these female speakers.[16] Most notable, however, was that all these female speakers, who raved about women's status in Islam and the importance of mothering, wore *hijab.* It was also striking that these female speakers were involved in academic or other insulated careers where they rarely encountered average Americans; it seems that they worked with other intellectuals and academics. On the other hand, Shahmim Ibrahim and Najma Adam, two women who are quite busy working on behalf of their advocacy organizations and women's shelters, do not believe in wearing *hijab.*[17] It seems that the more activist a woman is in the American sense the less likely she is to wear *hijab.* A conservative Muslim's idea of activism is captured by the speakers at the ICNE Conference: women who work in an insulated environment who consider parenting their main activity and wear *hijab.* As ICNE has no women on its executive committee, men decide which women's views are represented in the organization. As a result, men choose women with opinions that do not threaten their control. ICNE would never have chosen a female speaker who did not wear *hijab* because from the outset she would be challenging a doctrine handed down by men. However, ICNE can choose female speakers who wear *hijab* and are thereby conceding defeat in one area of male hegemony. Whatever else these covered women would say could not challenge the male members. As a result, women think they have a forum for discussion, and men can credit themselves for listening to a woman's view. The truth is that her view has already been stifled.

Instead of focusing on real problems and on Islam, American Muslims end up worrying about what a woman should wear. One woman who responded to Yvonne Haddad's and Adair Lummis's survey of immigrant Muslims in the United States said, "Men can wear what they please . . . but they are fussy about the clothing of women in the mosque."[18] Feminist Muslims are bothered by this focus, particularly when there is so much else to emphasize, such as Islam's view on human rights. Men's focus on *hijab* exemplifies "a male desire to control women." Robert Marquand quotes Muslim feminist Rabia'a Kiegler as saying, "[Men] should stop bothering women about what they put on their heads—as if that were more important than what is in their heads."[19] According to Haddad's and Lummis's survey, 47 percent, almost a majority, of immigrant Muslims disagree with the statement "Muslim women should not go out on the street unless their hair and arms are covered and their skirts are well below their knees."[20] Unfortunately, this group is not very vocal. It is downright shameful that some Muslim men in positions of power discredit the efforts of a Muslim woman because she does not wear *hijab*. It is embarassing that some American Muslim women's activism is not recognized as admirable because they do not agree with majority interpretations of Qur'anic passages. Najma Adam says,

> I don't wear it [hijab] because I don't think it's the external that counts. I think that if you carry yourself with modesty, and you have a clean heart . . . that . . . [is] more important to me . . . I've seen Muslims

who talk a lot . . . about, "Oh, Islam, this, and I'm a Muslim. You're
not wearing your hijab, and how dare you?" But you know what? I'm
the one who's in social work, and they're the ones who are making a
million dollars a year . . . so you're wearing your hijab, but what are
you giving back to the community? What are you doing for other
humans? . . . When I started studying about Islam. . . . I realized the
best way to practice Islam was to . . . [help] your fellow man. . . . It
wasn't about the money. It wasn't about [prayer] five times a day.[21]

From Adam's perspective, the men who say women must wear
hijab are the same ones who can offer no solution for the women
in her shelter, other than to purchase a ticket home for them.
From the American Muslim community perspective, Adam may
be too independent. The editors of *In Our Own Voices: Four
Centuries of American Women's Religious Writing,* Rosemary
Skinner Keller and Rosemary Radford Ruether, write:

> Independent women with careers are looked on with suspicion by the
> Muslim community. The Muslim woman who tries to live between the
> larger American culture and the Muslim subculture is in a double bind,
> made a visible "alien" by her distinctive garb on the job, while
> regarded as a "loose" woman by her community without such garb.

They add, "The Black Muslim woman becomes doubly set apart,
both from the African-American Christian and the white communities, defined by her dress as a hostile apostate from both
societies."[22] Wearing *hijab* is a nice idea, but *hijab* does not solve
the real problems of American Muslims; it exacerbates them. For
instance, some feel it is a status symbol with American Muslim
communities for a man to have a traditional wife, meaning a wife
who wears *hijab,* stays home, does not question decisions, and so
on.[23] Rasha El-Desuqi, one of the speakers at the ICNE
Conference, called on Muslim women to become professionals:
"We need our sisters to become doctors, lawyers so they can help
us. We don't want help from non-Muslims or brothers."[24] El-
Desuqi is practically suggesting that she cannot do it, and that it
is time for the line to be crossed. A first step, though, would be for
women like El-Desuqi to break the chain of patriarchy, that

manifests itself in the emphasis on *hijab* and marriage, and not insist that their own daughters marry young and wear *hijab*. African-American Muslim women are willing to give up their freedom for a secure marriage,[25] even as they are starting to bristle under the requirements of gender segregation at Islamic functions or even dinner parties at another Muslim's home.[26] It seems that more Muslim women are asking for a return to gender relations as they were in the Prophet's time, with women praying alongside men and not in a side or rear room.[27] "If Muslim women were treated only fifty percent of the way the Prophet asked, we would be making more progress," says Shireen Jaouni, a graduate student at the University of Maryland in College Park.[28]

Aminah McCloud offers the example of Clara Muhammad, who "tended the Nation of Islam in its early days when Elijah Muhammad was jailed or running from the police," and female founders of other African-American Islamic sects; nothing has been written about their lives.[29] These women are thus perceived by historians as unimportant to the movement, a view which is not true.

Most American Muslim women do not cover their heads,[30] but *hijab* and orthodox dress are gaining in popularity, especially among young women who strongly believe in the practice.[31] Those who talk about wearing *hijab* love it. Says Anis Ahmed, principal of the Sawtelle New Horizon School, "A Muslim woman is adorned by her simplicity and beautified by her modesty."[32] Nancy Hanaan Serag, a young Muslim woman, wears hijab because, ". . . I'm not judged on how short my skirt is or the color of my hair . . . I am judged for who I am."[33] A respondent to Anway's survey says she receives special treatment because she wears a head to toe cover: "I get special treatment everywhere I go . . . I get great seats on planes, people let me in front of them in lines, and sometimes merchants . . . will give me free gifts or free service."[34] Though special treatment is not the purpose of *hijab,* it turns out to be an added bonus; however, the woman quoted above probably does not have a job and, therefore, does not deal with job discrimination.

Kathy Dobie writes in her *Washington Post* article on Muslim women that those who dress modestly, with or without *hijab,* are respected on city streets.[35] *Hijab* prevents men from making covetous looks at the woman wearing it and, some feel, forces men to take the woman more seriously and not see her as an object.[36] Some see *hijab* as a way of "protesting American sexual immorality."[37] One woman even said that "sexuality blossoms behind the veil!"[38] Women who wear *hijab* insist they are not oppressed: "[I]t is not degrading to wear proper clothing . . . my husband does the laundry, helps with cleaning (even the toilet bowl!) and helps look after the children so I can go out."[39] *Hijab* allows one to focus, says Hayat Alvi, on "other important features in a person, such as morality and faith, intelligence, love and care."[40] One woman who covers her whole body says that Muslim women should dress in *hijab* so as to be able to identify fellow American Muslim women.[41]

There are women who wear *hijab* and would rather not, but they are coerced into silence: "My biggest battle," says one respondent to Anway's survey, "is the head covering. . . . Nobody knows this though, since I accept and submit to the covering for modesty reasons."[42] One reason not to wear *hijab* and Islamic dress is that it is uncomfortable.[43] And one of the most powerful reasons not to wear *hijab* is that one attracts attention as a result of wearing it; especially since, according to the male Muslims who rally for it, the whole point of *hijab* is to keep oneself from being noticed.[44]

CLOSE-UP
We've Come a Long Way, Baby

American Muslims have undoubtedly come a long way, from obscurity and insecurity to an acknowledged presence on the American landscape. Like other large American communities, we are spread out all over the country. The largest concentration of American Muslims (about one million) lives in California, and constitutes a whopping 25 percent of the American Muslim population; these Muslims make up 3.4 percent of the state's total population. The next largest population of Muslims (800,000) lives in New York, making up 4.7 percent of the state's total population. The other populous Muslim states, in order, are: Illinois, New Jersey, Indiana, Michigan, Virginia, Texas, Ohio, and Maryland.[1]

The number of American Muslim organizations is large and growing. The organizations' purposes run the gamut from schools and places of worship, to media watchdog groups that work with media to rectify use of stereotypes of Islam, and Washington D.C. based organizations which work with Congress on legislation affecting Muslims. Across the country there are roughly 2,000 mosques in towns of all sizes. Of the 200 Islamic schools, about half are full time. Steven Barboza, an African-American convert, estimates that there are 200,000 businesses owned and managed by Muslims.[2] Muslims produce approximately 89 publications and have formed roughly 426 associations.[3] Many small organizations with specific purposes have been formed, such as to influence politics or deal with women's rights. For example, the American Muslim Alliance (AMA), a political organization, has branches in several states. The Muslim Public Affairs Council (MPAC), the American Muslim Council (AMC), and the Council on American-Islamic Relations (CAIR) also deal with politics as well as improving Muslims' media image. The major national Muslim organization is the Islamic Society of North America (ISNA).[4] In addition, smaller, newer organizations, founded by Muslims who were born to immigrant parents but grew up as Americans, such as American Muslims Intent on Learning and

Activism (AMILA) and the Council of American Muslim Professionals (CAMP) are becoming players in the multifaceted community. Organizations serving Native American and Hispanic converts are also on the rise, providing support and Islamic materials in Spanish.

The American Muslim community has literally grown from a small group of immigrant Muslims praying together in a makeshift mosque in the midwest, to a large group spread throughout the country. Muslims have come a long way since the mass conversions of African-Americans in the sixties and the immigration of world Muslims in the late sixties and early seventies. Islam wasn't recognized as an official religion by the U.S. government until 1952, when Muslims serving in the armed forces sued the federal government for the ability to identify themselves as Muslims. Almost twenty years later, in 1971, Muhammad Ali won a legal battle that went up to the Supreme Court, vindicating his right to claim conscientious objector status to the Vietnam War because of his beliefs as a Muslim. Now, about 10,000 Muslims serve in the armed forces. The Air Force has even appointed a Muslim chaplain, and the Army already has two Muslim chaplains.

Such fast growth in size and in national awareness makes one wonder how the American Muslim community will grow in the future. In addition to gaining more influence, a significant factor in the next phase of community growth will probably be the taking over of the reins of mosques and other organizations by those Muslims who have lived here all their lives, Muslims born and raised here. Currently, immigrant Muslims tend to dominate leadership of the large American Muslim organizations like ISNA and CAIR. While they have done a fine job, it is time for the leadership of these groups to reflect the community's diversity, particularly by including those Muslims who have grown up in America.

Some Muslims are turned off by Islamic organizations that emphasize issues of importance to immigrants. Clearly, African-Americans would feel alienated, and people like me who grew up here sometimes chafe under some immigrant attitudes. When I attended my first ISNA convention, I mostly remember being told to stay away from American culture and to preserve our Islam by immigrant Muslims with more than their share of gray hairs. In one speech, the speaker vehemently emphasized that American culture was bad for us and announced that we should stay away from "MTV American culture." My sister and I looked at each other with some embarrassment. We had just been watching MTV in our hotel room! I recognize that living in the country my parents came from, Pakistan, wouldn't keep me away from MTV. They have satellite television too! And what about MTV Asia? I also know that living in Pakistan might not make me a better Muslim than I am here. Besides which, I am American and don't intend to move back, physically or mentally.

My attitude is that I, and other Muslims, are figuring out how to live as Muslims *and* Americans, not one or the other. Some immigrant Muslims may have a different attitude. They may see their home country as their ideal, while I see my country, the United States, as the ideal. African-American Muslims probably have similar feelings. I think there are positive aspects of American culture that help us to be better Muslims: the emphasis on gender equality, an ethic of hard work, involvement, and activism in the community. Right now, the children of the Muslim immigrants of the sixties and seventies are reaching adult age and, along with young African-American Muslims, want to be leaders not only in their communities but in America as well.

I think American Muslims will start seeing *themselves* as leaders. They will become more active and stop looking to mosques to support the community. In addition, American Muslims will not be ashamed to take time out of work to pray or take a day off from work because it's Eid (Eid al-Fitr, the major Islamic holiday ending Ramadan, the month of daily fasting, or Eid al-Udha, the second Islamic holiday, commemorating Abraham's faithfulness, specifically his sacrifice of a lamb instead of his son). They will do these things mostly because they want to fulfill their Islamic duties but also because they want other Americans to accept their religion. They want to show that they are Muslims in their behavior and that they are not ashamed of being Muslim in the same way that Christians are not ashamed to take off from work for Christmas or to go to church to pray. For as much as the American Muslim community has grown, we will need to grow even more to accomplish goals we have set for ourselves, particularly dispelling stereotypes about Islam and gaining acceptance of our religion.

─── *3* ◆ Jesus and
      Jihad ─────────────────

Muslims of different countries bring local culture to religious teachings, nearly creating their own branch of Islam. The essence of Islam is captured in the Qur'an, but the interpretation of the Qur'an is influenced by two things: native culture and a country's Islamic scholars, called the *ulema*. You might think native culture would not be so influential as to cause a religion to differ strongly from country to country. But this is the case.

For example, in Colorado, where I grew up, many people really value their right to bear arms, as specified in the Second Amendment. In Massachusetts, where I went to high school and college, people tend to focus on issues such as First Amendment rights of free speech. In California, where my grandparents live, people are more individualistic and focus on other aspects of the Bill of Rights. Such varied interpretation, or focus on particular aspects, is what happens with Islamic beliefs.

Each country has a tradition and a culture that pre-date Islam, and influence how those Muslims practice Islam and what they emphasize. For example, have you noticed how Catholic nuns, at least the traditional ones, cover their heads, sometimes their whole bodies, and look a lot like women from Arab countries who cover from head to toe? Obviously, nuns didn't pick this up from Muslim women. Actually, evidence suggests that women in pre-Islamic Arabia wore the head cover, the *hijab*. In addition, European women of the Renaissance era wore head covers to signify that they were important, or of the upper classes. *Hijab*, though practiced by Muslims, is probably a left-over of pre-Islamic Arabian culture.

Regardless of the country, all Muslims adhere to the Five Pillars, which are quite clear and do not require much interpretation (see the second Close-Up accompanying this chapter). The Qur'an and other sacred texts of Islam are complex and open to interpretation.

A major difference between world Muslims and American Muslims in interpreting the Qur'an and other texts is that in America there is no *ulema* (group of religious scholars) leading the Muslims, as there is in each Islamic country. Rather than turning to religious teachers who base their opinions on fourteen centuries of interpretation, American Muslims must solve their own theological problems from their own perspectives. As a result, some immigrant American Muslims may have become more actively and consciously religious than they would have been in their home countries. They begin interpreting the Qur'an and other religious literature themselves when they have a question, as opposed to consulting the local scholars, simply because there are none available.

The use of the word *jihad* exemplifies the differences between world and American Muslims. In the Middle East, where a country's leadership is defined by its stance against American hegemony, *jihad* has come to mean the struggle against Western countries' influence and power in the world, and particularly against America, which is perceived as bent on destroying the Arab way of life. Some Middle Eastern Muslim countries like to portray controversies as Islam versus America. In truth, the debates are usually over politics and arguably non-Islamic culture. I should point out that by no means does *jihad* imply terrorism, death, or holy war.

In America, Muslims understand *jihad* for what it really means: struggle. That's right, *jihad* merely means struggle, not a holy war or a war against all Americans. Consistent with the Qur'an and Prophet Muhammad's life, it often applies to an inner struggle to strengthen one's beliefs against corrupting and anti-Islamic forces. In America, *jihad* often means resisting the temptations of some aspects of life in America—like drinking or having sex outside of marriage, or just finding the time to pray five times a day.

Islam was founded on the same principles and ideas the United States was. Shocking as this may sound, Islam itself, though practiced by many in the East, is a part of the Western culture America is based on, with clear theories of right and wrong and belief in one God. When we say "Western culture," we mean peoples who see themselves as spiritual descendants of Abraham. Often, we'll hear politicians or scholars use the words "Judeo-Christian" to describe an ethic or value that is a part of Western culture. The two phrases, Western culture and Judeo-Christian, are almost interchangeable, in fact. What really lies at the heart of both phrases is monotheism. Western culture and the Judeo-Christian ethic are defined by a belief in *one* God, also the major belief of Islam.

The phrase really ought to be "Judeo-Christian-Islamic," however, for Islam is a part of the Abrahamic tradition and is strongly monotheistic. It is a little-known fact that Muslims believe that the Prophet Muhammad, the founder of Islam, was a direct descendant of Abraham, through Hagar's son Ishmael (Ismail in the Qur'an). The Qur'an also acknowledges the origins of Judaism and Christianity through Isaac, Ishmael's brother. In addition to their Abrahamic roots, the Torah, or Old Testament, and the Qur'an have similar stories and casts of characters. As Ishmael and Isaac were brothers, Muslims believe that Jews and Christians are their brothers, "Brothers of the Book," as they are called in the Qur'an. For that reason, Muslims are required by the Qur'an not to force Islam on others and to respect the rights of non-Muslims in freedom of worship.

So Muslims, Christians, and Jews have similar beliefs, similar holy books, similar teachings, and the same ancestral roots. Once we understand this, we realize the tremendous connection among these three religions: they are essentially tracks on the same railroad line. Granted, there are differences, but there are more similarities than we realize. These three religions exist on the same Judeo-Christian-Islamic trajectory as expressions of belief in *one* God. God is called Elohim or Yahweh in Hebrew, Lord or God in English, and Allah in Arabic. Doesn't it make you think that all Jews, Christians, and Muslims are praying to the same God if the only real distinction for the term "God" is what language it's spoken in?

Many people, nevertheless, refer to Islam as an Eastern religion. It is true that there are many Muslims who live in what we call the "East." However, Eastern religions (meaning non-Western ones) are actually religions or belief systems, more accurately, that are not monotheistic. Hinduism, for example, is an Eastern religion because it emphasizes belief in many gods and is not, therefore, a part of Western culture. Buddhism is also an Eastern religion and not a part of Western culture because it does not hold that there is one, omnipotent being. Eastern religions significantly add to our world's diversity.

People often make the mistake of calling Muslims "Muhammadans" after their beloved Prophet Muhammad. This term is incorrect, though, because it suggests that Muslims worship Muhammad as they would God.

Muhammad was God's mouthpiece on Earth. The Qur'an was revealed to Muhammad one day in AD 610, while Muhammad, who was forty years old at the time, was meditating in a cave on Mount Hira, near Mecca. The angel Gabriel (Gibreel in the Qur'an), the same angel that we read about in the Bible, came to Muhammad and compelled him to recite the word of God.

Muhammad, in my opinion, had one of the greatest mid-life crises known to humankind. Here he was, at the age of forty, reciting poetry as instructed by an angel. He ran home to his wife, Khadijah, and told her his story, thinking that he might be going crazy. He could not read or write. So how could he be a poet? Khadijah showed faith in her husband and asked him to repeat what the angel had told him, which is now the first *Surah* (or chapter) of the Qur'an. She recited it back to him: "There is no god but Allah, and Muhammad is his messenger." Khadijah became the first convert to Islam.

These revelations continued for twenty-three years, until Muhammad died around AD 632. God was sending His message to Earth through Muhammad, and Muhammad recited the beautiful poetry of the Qur'an, which was first recorded orally by his companions and later written down. Muslims believe that the Qur'an today has not been tampered with or altered, and each of the 114 *Surahs* or chapters is exactly the same as it was when Muhammad first began reciting it in Arabic in the cave near Mecca. The Qur'an is God's exact words, according to Muslims, which in order to be accurately understood must be read in the original Arabic. Translations will not necessarily capture God's exact meaning. As a result, many Muslims feel it their duty to learn Arabic and to read the Qur'an as God meant it to be read and heard. Translations of the Qur'an are not called "The Qur'an" but more often "The Meaning of the Qur'an," as translations are not exact replicas of God's words.

Besides sharing the story of Adam and Eve with the Torah and the Old Testament, the Qur'an also describes the Day of Judgment, the Resurrection of humankind, and the existence of Heaven and Hell. The Qur'an cites Adam, Noah, Abraham, Lot, Ishmael, Isaac, Jacob, Joseph, Job, Moses, Aaron, David, Solomon, Elias, Jonah, John the Baptist, and Jesus as prophets of Islam too, with Muhammad being the last prophet. The Qur'an, Muslims believe, is the final seal of God's earlier revelations to humankind as expressed in Judaism and Christianity.

Are you shocked at the similarities? It is especially surprising to read that Muslims believe Jesus was a prophet. Unlike Judaism, Islam acknowledges Jesus as a prophet of God, who taught His word on Earth. Jesus' life has taught me much, including the Christian stories about his love and kindness. We are all familiar with the Christian version of Jesus' birth, that the angel Gabriel told Mary that she would give birth to the son of God, that he would be the incarnation of God on Earth, the Son of Man, and she should name him Jesus.

> "Behold (O Mary!)" The Angel said, "God has chosen you, and purified you, and chose you above the women of all nations. O Mary, God gives you good news of a word from Him, whose name shall be the Anointed, Jesus son of Mary, honored in this world and in the hereafter, and one of those brought near to God. He shall speak to the people from his cradle and in maturity, and shall be of the righteous."

She said: "O my Lord! How shall I have a son when no man has touched me?" He said: "Even so; God creates what He wills. When he decrees a thing, He says to it, 'Be!' and it is."

Where do you think the above passage is from? The Bible? When I tell people about how Muslims view Jesus, I usually point out right away that we do not believe that Jesus was the son of God. My listener then naturally assumes that Muslims do not believe in the Virgin Birth either. Sometimes, he or she will even say, "You know, I always had trouble believing that Mary was a virgin."

I'll quickly add, "Muslims do believe in the Virgin Birth though." "Really?" people ask, shocked. Muslims believe that Mary, who is a very sacred woman in Islam with an entire chapter of the Qur'an devoted to her story, was a virgin, and that God chose her because of her unwavering faith, to mother one of his most beloved prophets. The Qur'an also says that God created Jesus as He created Adam: with His divine breath, He brought Adam and Jesus into existence. The above passage of good news from God is actually from the Qur'an, *Surah* 3, verses 42–47! Not the Bible!

So why don't we just say that Jesus is the son of God? It doesn't seem all that far off from what Christians believe, you may be thinking. It is a good question, with an answer that reveals the identity of God according to Muslims. Muslims believe that God is a being, omnipotent and without certain human qualities such as gender, though He is described as having eyes and a few other human features. Muslims believe He can create a person but does not bear offspring.

Nevertheless, God loved Jesus very much, so much so that he refused to let him die a gruesome death on the cross. Again, we are all very familiar with the Crucifixion story of the New Testament. Though as a Muslim I do not believe in that story, I am moved by it and can see how so many people feel passionately about it. The idea that God would give his only son to die for mankind's sins is the height of altruism and love. It is the essence of sacrifice: we must often give up things we love for a greater good. It almost makes me cry, thinking about Jesus' suffering on the cross for us and the humiliation he went through. I appreciate this story, but I do not believe it, as a Muslim.

Muslims believe that Jesus preached God's word throughout his life, and when he was betrayed by Judas, God could not let his prophet die in so horrific a manner. So God brought His hand down to Earth and lifted Jesus to Heaven. As a result, Jesus holds the distinction in Islam of being the only man to go to Heaven without dying. According to the Qur'an, Jesus shall return to Earth in some form, as a messiah, and will die an earthly death at that time.

Perhaps because of my upbringing, going to a Catholic grade school and a Protestant high school, I have always seen the three monotheistic religions as descriptions of different parts of a large painting or mural. We all see a section of it and think that it's the whole picture. Maybe, if we learned about each other's holy books—each other's sections of the painting—we might be able to see the whole painting and reach a more complete conception of God.

Anybody who learns about religion or is born into a religion has to wonder, "Which one is correct?" How can we all believe in God or a higher force, as with some Eastern religions, but have different holy books, rituals, and so on? If you are an intelligent person and are close to people who are not of the same religion, you must eventually come to the belief that each religion represents a different route to the same destination.

Though it's fine to believe this, I have always had a difficult time explaining that I believe we all pray to the same God in different ways. While most of the day in school I was a totally rational person who presented evidence for her arguments, when asked how I viewed religious diversity, I reverted to New Age–sounding talk of each person picking a path that was best for him or her, to reach the same place as everyone else in the end.

At Wellesley, Dean Kazanjian told us on the Multi-Faith Council about how he teaches kids about religious diversity. He arranges the group in a circle and places a large box in the middle. This box has drawings on it, painting too. Victor asks the kids to describe the whole box out loud. He wants to know what it looks like. But the catch is that they can't get up and walk around and look at the box. They can only shift in their seats and describe what they can see—some see corners; others see only the sides. Suddenly, the group realizes that the only way to describe the box is for all of them to share what they can see with each other. In the end, having heard from the kids next to them, across from them, and so on, and knowing what they can see from their own seats, the students know what the whole box looks like.

Most religions hold the belief that God, or the omnipotent being, is bigger than we are as humans, an omnipresent and therefore larger-than-life entity. So, if God is bigger than we are, wouldn't it be hard for just one of us to perceive Him? It would be like trying to see all of the moon's surfaces, even the ones facing away from us, on one dark night. But if a force or presence is bigger than we are, and we all tell each other what we can see of it, we have a shot at seeing or realizing the entire presence. When we try to see all of God by describing our religions to each other, we confirm our own faith and enhance our belief in God.

So what happens when Muslims immigrate to the United States from different countries with different cultures and mix with Americans, born and raised in American culture, who have converted to Islam? We end up with a new version of Islam: American Islam. What is American Islam? I believe it is a return to the Qur'an without the influence of pre-Islamic Arab culture. All of the cultural baggage must be set aside in an American mosque because it is very likely that not everyone is from the same country. Since they won't agree on rituals and practices determined by culture—such as whether men and women pray together or separately—and they don't have an *ulema* to settle the issue, they must decide for themselves and turn to the only guidance they have that is not culturally biased: the Qur'an.

As a result, I believe American Islam is a purer form of Islam than is practiced in some Islamic countries, because of the absence of cultural amplifications. If anything, American culture has influenced American Muslims to be better Muslims. For instance, following the example of American Christian and Jewish congregations that use their facilities as community centers, American Muslims also have made their mosques into family gathering places. In Islamic countries, mosques have not necessarily been community centers, and women and children have not attended for a variety of reasons. But now, in the United States the mosque has evolved into a place where American Muslim men, women, and children gather to pray and conduct other, community-strengthening activities. This is great for Muslims!

In addition, American Muslims have reread the Qur'an from an American perspective, paying special attention to passages that emphasize American values—self-respect and gender equality, among others. With Muslims in America, this is Islam's chance to prove its inherent compatibility with the West minus all the cultural baggage. Islam in America is Islam's chance to prove that it can stand the tests and rigors of time, change, technology, and culture.

American Muslims are making use of modern technology in their exercise of Islam's strong moral principles. For example, as an alternative to hearing the *adhan* (call to prayer) only in the mosque, American Muslims have created and adopted electronic watches with preprogrammed alarms to indicate the time of *adhan* (Casio's "Amazing *Al-Asr* Watch"), and they listen to audio cassette recordings and compact discs of Qur'anic recitations in their cars and on their Walkmans. American Muslims also have put the Qur'an and other Islamic texts on CD-ROM, the Internet, and television and video programs that spread the word of Islam in a way that has not been done before. This adaptation of Islam to modern forms of communication is changing the way Muslims learn and practice Islam.

My family was shocked and elated when Valli, my young cousin, who has trouble pronouncing some words, proclaimed upon hearing good news, "Subhan-Allah!" (Grace be to God!) Valli watches Islamic educational videos of a Muslim muppet named Adam that are produced by Sound Vision, an American Islamic production company. From Adam, Valli had learned the proper pronunciation and use of this Arabic phrase expressing God's greatness. When his parents settled in America, they had no idea that he would someday learn Islam through the "Barney medium."

With advances like Adam and the rediscovery of Islam's commonalties with Western culture, being Muslim poses less and less of a barrier to being American; in fact, being American makes it easier to be a Muslim and vice versa. As a result, American Muslims are achieving ever greater success in professional and personal life, accomplishments that benefit all Americans.

American Muslims believe in Jesus' message. As Jesus did his own *jihad*, teaching people the laws of the one and only God, American Muslims are doing their own *jihad* every day. They are trying to live God's words in their daily lives.

Good American Muslims are good American citizens. American Muslims want to coexist with their "Brothers of the Book" and all fellow Americans of all religions. They are waiting for the time when they are accepted as good citizens and fellow Americans by the rest of the country. I think Jesus would have wanted that!

CLOSE-UP
Jesus — Islam's Messiah at the End of the World

Every religion has a story about the end of the world, some more complex than others, but all of an ominous and powerful nature. Islam is no exception. The Qur'an describes the beginning of the end of the world: famine, storms, floods, vandalism, and rampant immorality prompting the arrival of Dajjal, the name of the anti-Christ in the Qur'an. Dajjal is described as a monster of God's creation, brought into existence by, and as an expression of, man's increasing savagery. As to be expected, events on Earth take a downward spiral with even more immorality and evil dominating the lives of people in the world.

Dajjal's reign of terror lasts only forty days, however, because God sends Jesus down from Heaven on a white horse with a lance in his hand to save the world for the righteous people—those who have lived their lives in service to God and with kindness to others. Jesus' throne will also be lowered to Earth from Heaven, and the faithful will rejoice upon seeing it. Jesus will lead an army of the righteous against Dajjal, who will be defeated by this army but will manage to escape. Nevertheless, Jesus finds Dajjal and kills him with God's lance.

Jesus will bring a reign of righteousness over the Earth for roughly eighty years. The Apocalypse and Judgment Day are still to come, though, with the death of Jesus. Jesus will return to Jerusalem, at the end of the period of his reign, and pray at the Dome of the Rock, dying and returning to God. Again, barbarism breaks out, and the angel of death, Azrail, shall come for the souls of the world.

Muslims vary on the *exact* details of the story of the end of the world in Islam due to a variety of interpretive approaches. However, most agree that Jesus, or at least a person who is a composite of Jesus and another holy figure, will return to the Earth as a messiah, as described above, and a savior of mankind. As a result, Jesus is one of Islam's most special prophets.

CLOSE-UP
The Meaning of the Five Pillars of Islam

Islam's basic beliefs are captured in what is called "The Five Pillars of Islam." They are almost like the sacraments in Christianity in that they capture the important aspects of the faith in a neat and concise way. Each pillar stands for a major tenet of Islam; the term Five Pillars is then like a mnemonic device.

The first pillar is called *shahadah*, which means "to bear witness," specifically to the belief that "there is one God, and Muhammad is His prophet." This is the most important pillar because it is the most basic belief a Muslim must hold. While all five pillars are important, this first one is key to a Muslim's existence. It is also the first chapter of the Qur'an. In order to convert to Islam, one must invoke the *shahadah* in the presence of another Muslim.

The second requires that all Muslims should pray to Allah five times a day. There is a funny story behind this requirement. In one of the chapters of the Qur'an, a journey of Muhammad's at night to Heaven to meet God is described. Muslims believe that there are levels of Heaven, with God occupying the uppermost level and persons occupying levels of Heaven according to how well they served God on Earth. Moses, who occupies the level just below God, counsels Prophet Muhammad when he returns from seeing God. Muhammad tells Moses that God has required Muslims to pray an exorbitant amount of times, something like 5000 a day. Moses persuades Muhammad that there is no way humans will be able to stick to that rule and that he must ask God for a more lenient prayer requirement. So Muhammad returns to God and explains that his people are imperfect and cannot be expected to pray so much. God agrees to lower the prayer requirement but to a still exorbitant number. Moses again persuades Muhammad to ask God to lower the number of required prayers, and God again lowers the amount. This interaction continues for some time until God lowers the prayer requirement to five times a day. Muhammad, despite Moses' exhortations, refuses to ask God for a further decrease. And so the second pillar of Islam was established.

The third pillar is called *zakat*, which means "giving alms." All Muslims who are able should give a portion of their yearly income to the needy. It is significant that *zakat* is included in Islam's central beliefs. Islam takes charity and compassion for others seriously. Muhammad himself was an orphan and bene- fited from charity. This pillar, along with other passages in the Qur'an, informs Muslims that part of their duty and identity as Muslims is to be compassionate and to give to those less fortu- nate. In Islam, you do not have to have money to perform *zakat*, you must simply be nice to others and do what you can. Prophet Muhammad said, "Even meeting your brother with a cheerful face is an act of charity."

The fourth pillar of Islam, and perhaps the most widely known, is *swam*. In the Islamic month of Ramadan, the month in which God began to reveal the Qur'an, obviously a very holy month for Muslims, Muslims abstain from food, drink, and sex from sunrise to sunset with the exception of those who are med- ically unable, women during the week of their menstruation or if pregnant, and those traveling. They can make up these days later in the year. This fast is required so that Muslims will learn self-control and cleanse themselves. Muslims are also supposed to learn what it is like for those who suffer from hunger. Muslims believe that prayers to God throughout this month and on par- ticular nights within this month will be given special attention by God. At the end of the month, Muslims celebrate Eid al-Fitr, a holiday equivalent in religious importance to Hanukkah or Christmas. Muslim families usually have a banquet and make a contribution to local poor people, usually a lamb sacrificed in God's name. Habiba Husain, a Muslim woman in San Francisco, feels charity is particularly important during Ramadan and stays quite busy with her organization, Rahima Foundation, delivering food to one hundred needy families during Ramadan and every month.[1]

The fifth pillar is called *hajj*, meaning "pilgrimage" in Arabic. Able Muslims are required, once in their lifetime, to go to

Mecca, the site of the Islamic shrine called the Kaaba, during the twelfth month of the Islamic calendar. Muslims perform particular symbolic rituals on this pilgrimage that are very interesting. First, pilgrims wear simple clothing so that any distinctions determined by clothing are eliminated. Second, they walk around the Kaaba seven times. The third ritual, walking seven times between the hills Safa and Marwa, reenacts Hagar's frantic search for water. Finally, the pilgrims stand as a group in the Arafat desert near Mecca and pray together to God for forgiveness. Imagine all those Muslims, of various races, black and white, from the third world and the first world, praying together, in their simple white clothing. Some people believe this event is a glimpse of the Day of Judgment when all humans shall rise from their graves and stand before God.

Muslims, however, should not perform this pilgrimage if doing so would bring harm to their families, such as leaving behind ill family members or selling one's home to pay for the trip. Those Muslims who have gone on *hajj* describe the event as inspirational and enlightening. In Mecca, Muslims of the world gather to pay homage to Allah. Since Muslims come from countries around the world and a variety of ethnic origins, Mecca is arguably the most ethnically and culturally diverse place on Earth.

— 4 ♦ Farrakhan's Choice: Militancy or Moderation —

O n my first day of ninth grade at boarding school, I was thrilled to see two more Islamic names on our class list: Ghani Salahuddin Raines and Umbreen Khalidi. I actually knew Umbreen from outside of school, but I was excited at the thought of meeting a Muslim I didn't know who wasn't a family friend or also attending a mosque event. Soon after I found the names, I was searching the mugshots of new students our school printed and distributed looking for my new Muslim classmate. Upon finding the picture, I did a double-take. Staring out at me from the black and white photocopy was a young black man. It looked as though the photographer hadn't given him much of a chance to smile—one of those photos where by the time you've turned around to face the camera, the photographer says, "Thank you," having shot you the moment you faced the camera and obviously weren't smiling.

But his expression didn't surprise me as much as did the fact that I had never known a black Muslim before. We eventually met and worked on projects together until we graduated. I used to joke with Ghani that if my parents went nuts and were about to force me into an arranged marriage with a scary, hairy monster, he and I would have to elope to save me, and I'd still be marrying a Muslim at least! For a long time, Ghani was all I knew about African-American Muslims. I even asked my mom one day when I was younger if our family, being American Muslims, were part of the Nation of Islam (NOI). She explained to me that the

NOI was a small group of African-American Muslims who had once followed Malcolm X.

Now I know that of the variety of ways Islam is interpreted and practiced in the United States, the Nation of Islam is obviously the most controversial. At the same time, the Nation of Islam could contribute to American society in a tremendous way. If we are to believe the estimates, NOI has only about 20,000 members, including a small number of NOI Muslim prisoners. Though members of NOI call themselves Muslims, NOI doctrine differs with Islamic doctrine on practically every important Islamic belief. Most African-American Muslims are actually Sunni Muslims like me. NOI Muslims are a different group entirely.

In fact, to many Muslims, NOI members are Muslims in name only. They subscribe to what one could call a corrupted version of the Five Pillars, more suited to worshipping Wallace Fard (also referred to as W. Fard), one of NOI's founders, who is revered as an incarnation of Allah. Islam strongly condemns such *shirk*—a person's claim to being God. The claim that Fard is God makes NOI highly suspect to Muslims. The additional creative freedoms NOI has taken with the Qur'an, such as the five daily prayers not being required, also trouble many Muslims. Today, we draw a distinction between Islam as described in the Qur'an and "Farrakhanism," the NOI version of Islam propounded by Louis Farrakhan, the leader of NOI. At the same time, we do not condemn them because we believe that is God's job.

A core belief of NOI is that Africans are the superior race. Islam, on the other hand, stresses equality among races. In fact, this emphasis originally was very attractive to African-Americans and in the sixties was one of the reasons many converted. Any visitor to Mecca is moved by the racial diversity of the Muslims on pilgrimage: white, black, South Asian, Asian, European, and more. However, Wallace Fard and Elijah Muhammad, the founders of NOI, seem to have taken the Qur'anic emphasis on racial equality too far and added their own beliefs that the African race is superior. In time, NOI leaders attacked whites, calling them devils and singling out Jews, in particular, and blaming the problems of African-Americans on them.

At one time, NOI's primary aim was to foster a middle-class lifestyle among African-Americans wholly separated from whites, including school, business, and social activities. Although that objective is downplayed now, because of it, NOI is very structured, almost militarily so. Sonsyrea Tate says in her book about her experiences as a member of the NOI, *Little X: Growing Up in the Nation of Islam:* "School, like everything else in the Nation, was serious business."[1]

The real aim of NOI doctrine as created by Elijah Muhammad, in my opinion, was to boost the morale and confidence of African-Americans following it. That would explain why much of the doctrine, like fasting during Christmas as opposed to during Ramadan is in response to and presented as an alternative to American Christian culture. I think Elijah Muhammad must have said to himself, let me work on my community's internal confidence and viability first. Tate writes in *Little X* that NOI schools made the young NOI members feel good about themselves: "Now that Elijah Muhammad had convinced them that they weren't hoodlums but children of God, they were absolutely fearless."[2] When that confidence and stability were established, Muhammad would have dispensed with the superiority and separatism talk because his community would be strong enough to function in society successfully, having been strengthened by years of isolation and self-discipline. NOI doctrine was only meant to last until the goal of community viability was achieved. The action of Elijah Muhammad's successor, his son, Warith Muhammad, seemed to bear out this theory. After taking over leadership of NOI, Warith Muhammad declared in 1975 that NOI would no longer be known as NOI or practice NOI beliefs. Instead, they were to become regular Sunni Muslims. (Currently Warith Muhammad refers to his community as the "American Muslim Society" for purposes of clarity and at the community's request.) Farrakhan, probably disgruntled at not being chosen by the Muhammad family to succeed Elijah and disagreeing with Warith's ideas, eventually revitalized the old NOI on his own in 1977, though with a much smaller following.

There is a lot more to NOI than the controversy over its rhetoric. The connection between Islam and African-Americans is, at first blush, a curious one: why were these black men and women attracted to Islam and Elijah Muhammad? What was it about Islam, this religion perceived to be exotic and Eastern, that appealed so much to so many African-Americans that they, of their own volition, converted from Christianity? It doesn't make much sense if you haven't studied the civil rights era in America or aren't familiar with Islamic teachings.

Islam, for those African-Americans during the civil rights era who chose to convert, was a means of liberation and freedom from their low status in society. African-Americans faced severe discrimination and, though free, were still seen by many as slaves. Many were poor, suffered from prejudice and racism as represented by Jim Crow laws and segregation. Black people were *required by law* to sit at the back of buses and drink from specific water fountains in states like Alabama and Mississippi. They could eat only at specified restaurants. Even laundromats were segregated! As if such legalized racism wasn't shameful enough, lynchings and other physical abuse of African-Americans happened as well. The Ku Klux Klan was thriving. Yet, when black people went to church, ministers and priests told them to turn the other cheek. They were told that for their suffering, they would inherit the Earth.

Forgiveness, passive resistance, and loving one's enemy has its place, and I find that it takes a strong person to adopt those values as themes for their entire lives. Jesus believed that one could change the world with love, and I find that very moving and brave. The essence of moral bravery is to love one's enemy despite his faults and his antagonism toward one's cause and people.

However, the situation many African-Americans faced in the 1960s was intolerable, and the message of forgiveness that Christian preachers put forth did not fill the void for many of them. It was in this environment that today's NOI, though founded with curious origins by Fard in the 1930s, emerged. If I were in a similar position, and Elijah Muhammad came to me and said, "You don't have to keep taking this abuse. You can improve your life with discipline, hard work, and education. We can stand up to the people who are abusing you," I would certainly sign up with him and NOI. A number of African-Americans, from the 1960's on, have studied Islam and converted to Sunni Islam of their own volition as well because they were also attracted to the teachings of Islam.

Islam gave those who converted self-respect. While Islam believes in forgiving one's enemies and prefers making peace when possible to making war, Islam does not advocate succumbing to one's own suppression. That message of Islam—self-improvement—resonated with those African-Americans seeking self-empowerment. The life of the Prophet Muhammad itself is inspiring for those beaten down by society. He overcame his inadequacies—he was illiterate, an orphan, and poor—to become a successful businessman with a large, loving family. He also became one of the greatest world leaders, maybe the greatest ever.

Islam never indoctrinated people with ideas or principles justifying one racial group's superiority over another. There is no chosen or preferred race of people in Islam. A well-known passage of the Qur'an is often cited as promoting racial harmony and the importance of diversity. The passage says that God actually divided His people into races (or tribes, as sometimes translated from the Qur'an) and nations so that we would have a way of identifying each other. The identification and association of people with certain cultures and from particular areas of the world would (and should) then facilitate a means of meeting and acquainting ourselves with each other. If we were not organized in this manner, would cultural exchanges and an appreciation of difference be possible? It is thus a wonder to me that all African-Americans did not convert to Islam! The message of Islam, especially of gaining self-respect, was and is very relevant to African-Americans and other marginalized groups today.

So, great—NOI gave some African-Americans self-respect. But why do mainstream Muslims like me tolerate Farrakhanism with its racism and other un-Islamic principles? The truth is that Muslims do not believe that Farrakhanism is a proper interpretation of the Qur'an. However, Muslims are instructed by the Qur'an not to judge each other because only God can pass judgment, and He will do so on Judgment Day. The most exciting development in Farrakhanism is Farrakhan's February 2000 pledge, reconfirmed at a gathering of Muhammad's followers on the 2000 Labor Day weekend, with Warith Muhammad to unify their communities, ending twenty-five years of rifts.[3] Farrakhan has also declared the *shahada* at these meetings, thereby, in effect, rejecting NOI's racist ideology. Similarly, Farrakhan reformed NOI observance of Ramadan and prayers on Friday, bringing NOI more in line with Islam.[4] If Farrakhan is really serious about abandoning Farrakhanism, the results could be phenomenal. Some suggest that Farrakhan's recent bout with prostate cancer has brought about his changed views and that he is now newly committed to unity and harmony. A unified group of African-American Muslims, in the view of NOI leaders, could embark on large projects to reform America's poorest neighborhoods where they have ties and influence.[5]

But American Muslims are so excited about a reunion of the two sides that no one has stopped to ask if Farrakhan really is ending Farrakhanism. The differences that caused the original split, about Islamic theology, have not been totally resolved.[6] Another not well-known truth is that NOI's radical messages cloud their positive deeds that benefit all of society. You may be wondering what NOI could contribute that American society would want to adapt. Had I not researched the topic, I would wonder too—what could a racist, anti-Semitic, separatist group possibly have to contribute to the United States?

But I have to admit that once I disregard their racist rhetoric, I realize that the NOI is responsible for positive change in its communities. Farrakhan is a good American citizen for helping African-American communities in the inner cities. I think his racism is unfortunate, but I try to distinguish that from the contributions his organization has made. In that sense, NOI is practicing at least one Islamic pillar, that of *zakat,* or charity. In addition, NOI pays particular attention to Qur'anic provisions on having a presentable appearance and conducting oneself in a disciplined manner. So, rather than wholly condemn NOI, I support their actions that are Islamic and positive, I am against their racist doctrines, leaving the final judgments to Allah.

Those who live in the Paradise Manor and Mayfair Mansions neighborhoods of Washington, D.C., near the Maryland border, have seen their neighborhoods, at one time overrun with crime and inner-city violence, rehabilitated by NOI. Now the communities are safe and without heavy drug activity.

It began quietly. NOI members, under the direction of Dr. Abdul Alim Muhammad, NOI pastor, spokesperson, and health minister, began selling copies of the NOI paper, the *Final Call,* in a neighborhood classified in 1987 as one of the ten most active drug-trafficking zones. The drug dealers were surprised and disturbed by the NOI members and actually left the neighborhood when they were there. A few residents noticed this trend and had the idea that if NOI patrolled the area, their influence might cause a decrease in crime. They asked the Fruit of Islam, NOI's security arm, if they would be willing to patrol, and a partnership between NOI and inner-city communities began.

NOI denies that its members try to intimidate or threaten the drug dealers in the neighborhoods they patrol. They simply do what they are authorized to do by residents: ask people who look out of the ordinary if they live in the neighborhood and, if they don't, ask them to leave. I would argue that the appearance of the Fruit of Islam alone is intimidating: members wear a uniform of a suit and bow tie, and they are always standing at attention. Obviously it works. NOI's efforts in Washington, D.C., were recognized in 1992 by Mayor Sharon Pratt Kelly, who declared July 11 "Abdul Alim Muhammad Day."

In addition, the prisoners converted by NOI, though fewer than Sunni Muslim converts, may stay out of jail permanently and function in society with NOI's assistance. NOI has a strong tradition of education. In spite of some misguided ideas about coeducation (specifically, NOI wants to separate boys and girls in school, not so that girls might receive equal education but so that girls are protected from boys, thereby invoking and enforcing a patriarchal principle that becomes self-fulfilling), NOI schools have educated many African-Americans who are professionals today. They owe some of their success to NOI even though they may no longer be members or are now part of Warith Muhammad's Sunni Muslim African-American community.

Louis Farrakhan can preserve these positive aspects of his legacy if he takes NOI into the mainstream. But will he? It would mean abandoning some aspects of his philosophy, specifically the racist, anti-Semitic, and separatist rhetoric. None of these is important to his movement.

First of all, the racist rhetoric is un-Islamic. Farrakhan probably realizes this and knows he is using incendiary remarks to prove larger points and gain credibility in his own community. I don't think he is racist at his core, rather he sees rhetoric as a means to an end. He should realize that his community does respect him, regardless of such rhetoric, and more people, like me, would take him seriously if he stopped deluding himself and others with Jewish conspiracy theories.

Second, founding his own nation, a NOI goal, anywhere in the world is a ridiculous idea. Why would anyone want to leave behind the successful American economy for a non-existent one, especially now when minorities really can succeed in American society? Farrakhan, as a result, rarely brings up separatist arguments.

Farrakhan faces pressure to take NOI mainstream, because of its small size and its decreasing appeal as revolutionary fervor dies down in the African-American community. The NOI community, of about 20,000 members, may seem larger merely because Farrakhan is so vocal that he appears to be leading a gigantic group. He frequently appears on television and is written up in newspapers after public appearances. In truth, Farrakhan is walking loudly and carrying a small stick. NOI's small size wouldn't be a problem if Farrakhan could count on the movement growing, if it were guaranteed that Elijah Muhammad's message of self-respect and black superiority would have appeal for the ages.

However, I predict that the NOI is not going to grow but probably shrink if its message remains unchanged. The message is based on a revolutionary fervor, a need to turn one's back defiantly against the system. But the time for that fervor has ended. We no longer have Jim Crow laws, and African-Americans hold prominent positions in society. The good fight has been fought, and now African-Americans are looking for other kinds of fulfillment. Like Malcolm X, many members may become disenchanted with NOI and Elijah Muhammad's teachings. Once they have dealt with their passions against the system that oppressed them, and sit down to read the Qur'an, they realize that Sunni Islam is more satisfying for them than NOI doctrine. For this reason Farrakhan would be smart to merge what is left of his NOI with the rest of the American Muslim community while he still has some members.

Reading the Qur'an makes one realize the faults within NOI doctrine. The Qur'an states that the Prophet Muhammad is the seal of the Prophets, the last messenger from God to mankind. Yet, NOI claims that Elijah Muhammad was a messenger of God as well, which doesn't make sense from a Qur'anic viewpoint. For Malcolm X, it was the discovery of Elijah Muhammad's affairs with multiple women, his fathering of their children, the later denial that he was the father, and overseeing the expulsion of these women from the Nation, that caused Malcolm X to be disenchanted with NOI. After Malcolm X went on *hajj* (the required pilgrimage to Mecca) and prayed alongside Muslims of all colors, including white Muslims, he realized that he had been practicing NOI Islam and not Qur'anic Islam: "For 12 long years I lived within the narrow minded confines of the 'straightjacket world' created by my strong belief that Elijah Muhammad was a messenger direct from God Himself, and my faith in what I now see to be a pseudo-religious philosophy he preaches."[7] He preferred true Qur'anic Islam in the form of Sunni Islam. I do not think Malcolm X's experience is unique.

This is the pressure that Farrakhan faces—now that the NOI has made its point in American society about the mass disenfranchisement of African-Americans—will its members start looking for real spiritual fulfillment in real Islam? The question Farrakhan must ask himself is: Am I going to be Sunni Muslim and let the truth of the Qur'an guide me and my community, or am I going to be a political leader, an ideologue, with influence, limited as it may be, living off homespun tales of Allah on Earth and white devils that are little match for the beauty and honesty of the Qur'an? Farrakhan must choose between sole power and control versus the truth he probably feels in his heart. The numbers show that NOI members, like Malcolm X, have walked away from the NOI when they realize what Islam really is. Is Farrakhan going to go down with this ship and its few passengers or save it and live to dock again?

Louis Farrakhan knows that he can help Americans. He once gave a speech to Congress saying that he deals with the lowest of America's low—the drug dealers and career welfare recipients— and that he can reform them, a job most Americans aren't willing to take on. Many Americans may say that they would rather be rid of Farrakhan and they hope that his movement dies out. On the other hand, Farrakhan's programs would be invaluable to this country if only he would put his talent to the country's benefit. Changing his spots would mean some obscurity and less absolute power for Farrakhan. I fear, though, that if he tries to preserve his power and NOI as it is, he will lose his followers. His innovations, *which positively affect American society,* will regretfully die with him.

If Farrakhan would forsake the racist rhetoric and say, "NOI shall now follow Sunni Islam, like the vast majority of American Muslims," the impact would be tremendous. Muslims like me could accept Farrakhan's innovations wholeheartedly. We could even become a part of his team. American Muslims could form a Muslim Americorps, a network of volunteers devoted to cleaning up America's worst neighborhoods based on Farrakhan's strategies. Wouldn't it be great if Congress could endorse a community clean-up program based on his successful model? What if

Farrakhan could bring the NOI emphasis on education to the inner cities and African-American communities? Farrakhan has solutions for the problems of America's ghettos. But we, as Americans, need to be able to trust him before we will endorse him to deal with these problems. We should all hope for Farrakhan to realize that the time for NOI-style revolution has ended. Now all of America deserves to *benefit* from his leadership.

There are signs that Farrakhan is thinking about taking his NOI mainstream, as Warith Muhammad did when he inherited leadership of the group upon the death of his father, Elijah. Farrakhan has had dialogues with Middle Eastern leaders and American Sunni groups like the Islamic Society of North America (ISNA). He has said in public the *shahada*, proclaiming that there is only one God and that Muhammad is his messenger, explicitly excluding Elijah or Fard from any divine status. If Farrakhan wants the positive aspects of NOI to survive, he probably knows that he must bring his group to follow Sunni Islam. He has certainly cut down on his racist, anti-Semitic rhetoric and has indicated that he is sorry for his controversial remarks and wants to move beyond them, particularly since the 1992 NOI publication of *The Secret Relationship between Blacks and Jews,* a book whose main thesis was that Jews were active participants and perpetrators of the slave trade. The book's scholarship is not held in high regard by academics.

His 1993 book, *A Torchlight for America,* exemplifies both Farrakhan's near total abandonment of classic but useless NOI objectives and his new emphasis on helping the larger American society. *Torchlight* addresses issues affecting all Americans, not just African-Americans, and is written with a thoughtful tone, clearly aimed at a mature, intelligent reader. The book is definitely a break from the usual NOI propaganda, particularly given the absence of separatism talk.

But Louis Farrakhan taking his movement mainstream won't mean a thing if Americans aren't willing to accept him and his movement. The question is simple: Are no values, as represented by the violence of life in the inner city, the lack of post-jail support for prisoners, and poor public education, better than Farrakhan's values, better than the Islamic values he espouses? Are Americans willing to let Farrakhan reform aspects of American culture? Will you, as an average American, accept him? Accept him in the way you have accepted the Reverends Billy Graham and Jerry Falwell? You might say, "I trust those men because they have proven their commitment to the United States, whether I agree with their ideals or not. But are Farrakhan's overtures of secularism really just a prelude to taking over our institutions and people?" Right now, Farrakhan must continue to show good faith to the American people so that he is not perceived as a threat.

Now it's up to you. Do you think Farrakhan is being sincere? He is certainly like the Greek god Janus with two faces. It is difficult for me to move beyond the face that called Judaism a "gutter religion" and praised Hitler, even though Farrakhan says those statements have been taken out of context. But we must try to see Farrakhan's other face, the one that talks about cleaning up America and elevating the status of the inner city and solving the social problems that affect Americans. The face that wants to contribute to a national dialogue on making America an even better place to live, the one that has a proven track record in that area.

For Farrakhan to be such an American leader, he must cease with useless, hurtful rhetoric. Some criticisms have their place but generalizations and intentionally hurtful statements are unbecoming in a leader of the stature Farrakhan would like to be. As much change as such a metamorphosis would require, Farrakhan needs to stop being a militant and become a moderate in order to bring his ideas to help America *to all Americans,* black *and* white.

CLOSE-UP
In *Shahada*: Conversion and Renewal in Prison from Malcolm X to Mike Tyson

The most famous American Muslim prisoner, without a doubt, was Malcolm X, who came to prison a pimp of the streets and left a proud member of the Nation of Islam (NOI). Malcolm, through conversion to NOI, discovered his own self-worth. All his life, up until prison, he had been only slightly better than dirt, according to his own estimation. He was sexually promiscuous, used drugs and alcohol, was dishonest and even sold women to other men. In prison, he realized that he had hit rock bottom. Elijah Muhammad's teaching reached him in prison, as NOI routinely preached to prisoners. Malcolm was suddenly emboldened by the realization of his own self-worth and his ability to pull himself up: this was what Islam said to him.

When he converted, he requested a new name for his new identity as a Muslim. When the letter from Elijah Muhammad came, it read "Malcolm X," for "X" was the name given until he proved to the NOI leadership that he deserved a Muslim name. To Malcolm, "X" not only replaced his former surname, Little, but also spelled out how his identity had been ripped away by slavery, making him an anonymous person. It also suggested that one was an "ex"-slave.

With the surname and the religion of the slaveowners that once owned his family gone, Malcolm became a warrior of words and speeches for Elijah Muhammad and perhaps NOI's most prominent and influential spokesman ever. Though less attention has been paid to them, the themes of his speeches and his ideas were extraordinary. If Elijah Muhammad is seen as the Jesus of his movement, Malcolm X then is Paul, blinded by the light of truth one day in prison and devoting the rest of his life to spreading that truth. Though his place in American history was secure, he became a real-life symbol of the evolutionary and dynamic nature of America, as his own views on Islam evolved from NOI's racist beliefs to a true Qur'anic Islam under which Malcolm embraced women and men of all colors.

How different America's civil rights era would have been had Malcolm X never existed. Someone might have emerged in his place, but I doubt anyone would have added to the debate as Malcolm did. Malcolm's speeches empowered the African-Americans who heard them, encouraging them to take pride in their identity and in their race. One need only watch a speech of Martin Luther King's and then one of Malcolm X's to realize that King, in his own right a charismatic and gifted speaker, seemed to speak to white America on race issues while Malcolm really spoke to black America. Malcolm's ideas lived on in his wife, Dr. Betty Shabazz, until her sad and untimely death in 1997.

The conversion of prisoners to Islam by Muslim religious groups is flourishing even more today than it did in Malcolm's time, and it has also taken on a different character. During Malcolm's time, NOI was the major Islamic group converting prisoners, to a racist brand of Islam that was barely in line with the Qur'an. (In the 1960s and early 1970s, black Muslim inmates, following the lead of civil rights leaders, won court decisions for increased individual rights in prison, such as requesting meals without pork.) Today, according to anecdotal evidence I have put together, the vast majority of prisoners are being converted to Sunni Islam by Sunni Islamic groups and called "in *shahada*," referring to Islam's first pillar, the *shahada* or declaration of faith to one God and His messenger, Muhammad.[1] The number of Muslims in American prisons was most recently estimated to be 300,000 to 350,000 in 1985, about 8 percent of the American Muslim population, with 90 percent of those prisoners being African-Americans. According to a 1991 American Muslim Council study, about 35,000 prisoners convert to Islam each year.[2]

Should we be frightened by this trend, or pleased about it? Many are actually quite pleased, from wardens to prison chaplains for other faiths. Dr. Aslam Abdullah writes in his *Minaret* magazine article "Ramadan in Prison" that "Don Simanski, a

Catholic chaplain finds Muslim prisoners showing exemplary behavior in their dealings with each other. 'I have had a great privilege of talking to Muslim prisoners and I have been very humbly impressed by their spirituality,' he said."

What is overwhelming is the increasing rate of prisoner conversions in the past ten years. When Pakistani immigrant Muslim Jan Muhammad Diwan started working with Muslims in California prisons ten years ago, as the result of a letter he read by a Muslim prisoner in a Muslim magazine, there were about 25,000 Muslims in prison, 15,000 of whom had converted in prison. Since then Diwan has retired from his job, devoting himself full-time to the organization he founded to assist Muslims in prison, the California Muslim Prisoners Foundation. His main activities are distributing Islamic materials like the Qur'an, prayer rugs, and skull caps, raising funds to buy Islamic materials, holding seminars for Muslim prisoners, and assisting with their fasting during Ramadan.

Today, says Diwan, 80 to 85 percent of Muslims in prison converted in prison, and the demand for Islamic materials like the Qur'an has grown tremendously. "In the beginning, I was excited to distribute twenty-five Qur'ans," says Diwan. "Today, I receive ten thousand donated Qur'ans and distribute them in a month!" He adds, "One Qur'an . . . takes the message [of Islam] to a thousand people [in the prison]" referring to the prisoners' habit of sharing Qur'ans.

Abdul Raouf Nasir, the state-paid imam to the Salinas Valley State Prison, also called New Soledad, near San Jose, California, says that Islam provides hope for prisoners. "In prison, desperation takes over, and opportunities close down. The humiliation of no privacy, isolation from family" causes prisoners to seek out something to give them hope, says Nasir. Judging from conversion rates, many prisoners find hope in Islam. Nasir adds that Islam may be especially resonant for today's prisoners because the African-American Muslim community has first-hand experience with the prison setting. Many black Muslims went to jail for refusing to comply with the draft for the Vietnam war, based on their Islamic beliefs. Warith

Muhammad, the leader of the African-American Muslim community, himself went to jail over the Vietnam draft. As a result, African-American Muslims can call on their memories and experiences of prison and apply their Islamic knowledge to rectify and soothe hardships of prison life for current prisoners.

Both Diwan and Nasir feel strongly that a very small number of Muslim prisoners are members of NOI. Diwan visits a large number of Muslims, 300 to 400 in some prisons, only 70 to 80 in smaller ones, and he only runs into "a few" NOI prisoners. He says that even these few prisoners eventually take *shahada* and rebuke NOI's racist beliefs: "The Nation of Islam opens the door to Islam." According to Nasir, at his Salinas prison the majority of Muslim prisoners, 200, are in *shahada,* and about 10 to 15 are NOI members. Most Muslim prisoners do enjoy hearing NOI's energetic speakers even though they disagree with their views and are not NOI members.

NOI prison ministry may be stronger in other states. For example, according to an article in the *Bay State Banner* newspaper, NOI has 20 prison outreach ministers for the Suffolk County House of Correction and other Massachusetts facilities.[3] The article did not say how many NOI followers were prisoners, however. I draw a big distinction between the work Diwan and Nasir are doing, teaching mainstream Islam, versus the alternative sects of Islam that are floating around out there, like the Five Percenters and the Moorish Science Moslems. They are not practicing mainstream Sunni Islam and are probably trying to exacerbate tensions within the prison community. Sunni Muslim prisoners, on the other hand, are known for their civility in prison and are the majority of prisoners.[4]

Some studies show that the rate of recidivism among Muslims is lower than any other group.[5] Nasir and Diwan also think that recidivism rates for the Muslim prisoners they have encountered must be low, though some do "make mistakes," Diwan says, and end up back in prison. They both cite the low recidivism rate as a result of community support from understanding Muslims and mosques for these prisoners. "I counsel them not to go back to their old neighborhoods so they can resist temptations," say Diwan, who also helps prisoners find jobs by preparing them for job interviews, buying suitable clothes for such an interview, and giving them a little money to help them commence their new lives.

Nasir feels that, due to federal and state budget cuts to such programs, the Muslim community has had to take on more responsibility in post-prison support services like opening halfway houses and assisting in job placement. Up until a few years ago, prisoners could receive state and federal funds for schooling. Now, mosques and Islamic centers are the only places Muslims can turn to for their education. For the most part, Muslim groups are answering this call. Of course they could do more, but in nearly every major American city, a small group of Muslim volunteers has organized to help prisoners begin rehabilitating themselves. Diwan told *Minaret* magazine, "I want to give each Muslim prisoner a copy of the Qur'an and prayer rug to make them feel happy and realize that people outside care for them and have not abandoned them for what they did in the past."[6]

In an attempt to garner credit for the efforts of Diwan, a man who has devoted his retirement to Muslims prisoners, I ask him how many Muslim prisoners he has helped in his ten years of grass-roots activism. Diwan sighs pensively and says, "I could brag and say, 'I've done all this.' [The truth is] Allah guided me to do that . . . [and] made it easy for me." Diwan's mission continues. He has more plans for helping the Muslim prison community.

This is great news for Americans. How many of us are willing to work with prisoners at all? Admirable people like Nasir and Diwan are really doing the dirty work, in the trenches with the downtrodden. The discipline of following an Islamic prayer schedule and Ramadan, the self-respect that Islam specifically gives prisoners, is exactly what some prisoners may need to succeed. Society benefits indirectly from the converted prisoners' rehabilitation. They become functioning members of society, holding jobs.

I would wager that with the help of people like Diwan and Nasir, many freed Muslim prisoners are reformed and no longer a threat to society. Some prisoners may go on to help their fellow downtrodden. Najee Ali, a self-proclaimed former gangster, converted to Islam in prison and, upon being set free, started an outreach program for the homeless of South-Central Los Angeles and those on skid row. The program, called "Project Islamic HOPE," which stands for "Helping Oppressed People Everywhere," clothes and feeds hundreds of people weekly.[7] It is nothing short of a miracle to me that the words of God, as recited by Muhammad fourteen hundred years ago in a lonely desert cave, are inspiring the male and female prisoners of America to live a better life beyond their cells.

── 5 ◆ Generalizations and Stereotypes: Muslims and the American Media ────────

L ike other Americans, I tend to generalize. I wonder how many of these generalizations that I and others subscribe to are influenced by what we hear from the media. Does the media influence us positively or negatively? Does the media have a responsibility to the public to be fair and to educate us?

Americans tend to associate all Muslims with the worst Muslim they know of at the time, a Muslim who is in the news for causing trouble. A situation where such oversimplification clearly hurt American Muslims and their efforts to be good citizens occurred in Loudoun County, Virginia, during the winter of 1997–98.

In early November, 1997, Saudi Arabian officials proposed the move of the Saudi Arabian-funded, full-time Islamic school, called the Islamic Saudi Academy, from Fairfax County, Virginia, to Loudoun County. The school had just lost a referendum vote by the residents of nearby Poolesville, Maryland, mainly because the school wanted to annex property in town, thereby avoiding a long, land-use review process in that county, and locals were against that. Some opponents had resorted to racist, anti-Arab rhetoric, yet the land-use issues remained central.

The current school was filled to capacity at 1,200 students and had a waiting listing of 1,000 more. The new school would accommodate 3,500, with about 200 slots going to local children,

Muslim or not. Most of the students at the new facility, as at the Fairfax County facility, are expected to be Americans (as opposed to Saudi nationals) who are Muslim, a fact that does not bother the Saudi Arabian officials. As an Islamic country, they feel they should share their wealth with Muslims all over the world who need assistance. The Islamic Saudi Academy serves scores of diplomats from Islamic countries, whose children can attend the school, as well as American Muslim children who can learn about their religion in a comfortable environment and gain confidence from being around other Muslims.

The Islamic Saudi Academy, which follows a Virginia-certified curriculum as well as teaching Islamic studies and traditions, thought that Loudoun County would be accepting of their plans. They had a great record with police and locals in Fairfax and needed only to be granted an exception by the Loudoun County Board of Supervisors to build a school on land zoned for ware-house use. The *Washington Post* wrote in November:

> Loudoun board Chairman Dale Pollen Myers . . . applauded the pro-
> posal, saying it could be an "exciting complement" to the growing
> communities in eastern Loudoun. . . . [S]ome officials predicted the
> plan would not encounter the opposition it received from Poolesville.
> . . . "I don't want to prejudge anything," said Loudoun Supervisor
> David G. McWatters . . . "but they certainly will not receive the kind
> of treatment they received in Poolesville."

These statements came to epitomize the term "famous last words" as the debate turned ugly. While some people had legiti-mate concerns regarding an increase in traffic and other land-use issues, such concerns in the school's proposed move were almost totally overshadowed by xenophobic, un-American, racist opposi-tion, directed mainly against Saudi Arabians but also against Muslims in general.

But none of this xenophobic opposition occurred until mid-December 1997, just as relations between Saddam Hussein and the United States were heating up. Many nightly newscasts led with stories on how the United States and President Bill Clinton might react to Saddam's arsenal of chemical weapons—an arsenal he had been stockpiling for years but that had recently caught the attention of the White House, the State Department, and the Department of Defense. Saddam consistently did not follow the guidelines for inspection of sites laid down by the United Nations, the United States, and other countries, and agreed to by Iraq at the end of Desert Storm. Suddenly, Americans stopped talking about whatever else they had been talking about and talked instead about Anthrax and chemical weapons Saddam might have. We also, as Americans, debated going to war with Iraq versus continuing diplomatic efforts.

Finally, we probably added yet another note of skepticism about Muslims into our minds—they can't be trusted: they bomb the World Trade Center, they build chemical weapons, they mistreat their women. This list could go on and on. Americans were and are right to be wary of *certain* Muslims, just as we are wary of certain extremist groups, or even wary of walking to our car alone across a dark parking lot late at night. Wariness, or fear, is often a good thing: it can motivate us to try harder, it is a warning to us that we might be in danger.

But many in Loudoun County forgot that we should fear Saddam Hussein, not an Islamic school whose primary population is kids. Though town officials did not expect residents of Loudoun to put up a fight as the situation with Saddam and Islamic Iraq escalated, many showed how prejudiced they were against Muslims and how many stereotypes they hold of Muslims.

First, in mid-December, a flier, with no listed author, was left at some homes in Ashburn (the town in which the school would be located), warning residents that "thousands of Middle Eastern strangers [would be] roaming our streets while we work," as the Islamic Saudi Academy would "bring Muslim and Arab terrorists to Loudoun County." The Islamic Saudi Academy was billed as a terrorist training ground, a preposterous conclusion considering the school's stellar record in Fairfax.

One female protestor wore a body-cover, similar to the cover Saudi Arabian women wear, to a public hearing on the issue, and somehow claimed that by allowing the Islamic Saudi Academy to be opened here, women on American soil would be forced to wear this dress—"Islamic fashion police" she called it. Others said that Ashburn women and girls would suffer, as if the Academy employed misogynists who would force their opinions on the town. Reverend James Ahlemann, whose own Christian Fellowship Church had opened a parochial school without incident in recent years, opposed opening a school for Muslim children on the grounds that Saudi Arabia indulged in human rights abuses, not allowing non-Muslims to practice their religions in Saudi Arabia.

While Ahlemann and others were correct that Saudi Arabia does not have a stellar human rights record, opponents seemed totally to forget that the Board of Supervisors was examining land-use issues regarding a school for children, the majority of whom are U.S. citizens, at the school's current location, *in the United States.* How could a school, even if funded by the Saudi Arabian government, assert their misguided policies, which incidentally are not even close to what the Qur'an says regarding women and those of other faiths, on the rest of the community? In one example of sensible media commentary, *Washington Post* writer David Nakamura noted in his article, "Warnings and Welcomes: Muslim School Plan Divides Loudoun":

> Much of the rhetoric by opponents of the proposed school has been aimed at Saudi Arabians and others from the Middle East, but Islam is a religion followed by people in many countries, not just the Arab world. The Islamic Saudi Academy's existing facility has Muslim students whose families come from 35 countries.

Hysteria settled on Loudoun County as Ahlemann and others attempted to provide intellectual justifications for bigotry. Some requested voter referendums because locals' high emotions deemed that necessary, despite the fact that two Christian parochial schools had opened recently without any fuss. Others opposed the school on the grounds that it would be tax-exempt, ignoring that the aforementioned parochial schools were also tax-exempt, and that a facility that could be taxed on the site—a warehouse, which the location was zoned for—would generate about fifty times more traffic than the Islamic Saudi Academy's seventy buses would! To me, the xenophobia the Islamic Saudi Academy faced in its proposed move was the clear result of distorted media representation of Muslims. The media consistently fails to make a distinction between Muslims who do bad things and Muslims who follow the Qur'an.

Julia Duin wrote in the *Washington Times* that the Board of Supervisors should "Tell the Saudis they are welcome to expand their $50 million school here with one condition: A $50 million church, synagogue, Buddhist temple or whatever will be constructed within 30 miles of their capital city by whichever American organization can come up with the money first."

Duin's perspective is interesting, but I'd point out again, *this is America!* What if Canada told us that they had had it with our polluted air floating over to them and that we must cut down our oil consumption or else they will never let Americans come to Canada again? What if France told us that they were tired of Hollywood sending pointless comedies to their country, which are watched by many French people, thereby hijacking French culture, and, if we want to send our films there to make money, American theaters had better start showing just as many French films? What if the entire world demanded that for every McDonald's outside the United States a fast-food restaurant featuring that country's cuisine be opened in an American town?

Carbon emissions, *There's Something About Mary,* and Chicken McNuggets do not represent the American spirit (thankfully!). Likewise, the doings of the Islamic Saudi Academy will have no detrimental effect on American values. Fortunately, some Loudoun County residents realized this and reacted sensibly. Norman Schwarzkopf wrote a letter supporting the school's proposal to move, saying that xenophobic protests go against the ideals we fought for in Desert Storm. Kathryn Kern-Levine, a courageous woman, encouraged her Loudoun County neighbors to display a crescent and star, Islamic symbols, in their windows to welcome the school and its pupils. She said, "I want Muslims who move into Loudoun County not to feel scared."

A February 2, 1998, editorial in the *Richmond Times Dispatch* suitably addressed the attempts at justification of xenophobia:

> Such talk is not only repugnant but idiotic. (Reports of American children gunned down by terrorists using the current Fairfax school as a firebase have not exactly been saturating the newspapers and airwaves.) . . . Meanwhile, the best way to change the nature of Saudi government is to show its children the value of religious tolerance and cross-cultural respect.

The glimmers of hope in all this is that many sensible Americans did not lose their minds and perceive the Academy as a threat, *and* the Board of Supervisors did vote, 7-2, to approve the move. (However Muslims in the Chicago suburb of Palos Heights have faced similar discrimination and use of zoning and property laws against them in their attempts to open a mosque in that town.)[1] They considered land-use issues, although one of those who voted against cited Saudi Arabia's human rights abuses, comparing approval of the move (brace yourself) to giving a day-care license to a child molester! Adel A. Al Jubier, a high-level aide at the Washington Saudi Arabian Embassy, told the *Washington Times* that debate was characterized by discrimination against Muslims: "Would people stand for this if they were attacking another racial or ethnic group . . . I doubt it."

What effect does NBC Nightly News have on Americans? Does a television or newspaper article really affect us? I think it does and, in this case, for the worse. An American Muslim Council (AMC) poll found that the most disliked religious group in America was Muslims.[2] I'm the first to admit that some extremist Muslims, people whom I don't consider to be in the same community with me, have done very bad things—like taking hostages in Iran and bombing the World Trade Center in New York. However, most members of the media emphasized Islam a little too much in reporting on these and other stories. One newscast or article can crystallize a single image, be it accurate or inaccurate, for thousands of people.

I personally have never seen a newscast that makes Muslims look good, though I know most Muslims are good. Mike Wallace, Tom Brokaw, Dan Rather, and Walter Cronkite didn't say, "Not all Muslims are like this." I guess reporters thought that they weren't simplifying Islam. But they were, intentionally or not, reducing Islam to the worst view we can have of it.

Edward Said, a highly respected English literature professor and Middle East affairs commentator, says in his book on media coverage of Islam, *Covering Islam,* that by using academics and so-called experts, media reports give viewers and readers the idea that they understand Islam.[3] The news media doesn't point out that these experts often use biased material, says Said. An alternate viewpoint isn't presented, and the viewer is convinced that all Muslims are fundamentalist terrorists. In addition, Said writes that Islam is "a kind of scapegoat for everything we do not happen to like about the world's new political, social, and economic patterns."[4] As a result, the media can resort to blanket generalizations about Islamic countries that American media and Americans feel free to use as fact.[5] In effect, we have no accurate understanding of Islam.

So what if stereotypes are used? We use stereotypes of many groups. But inaccurate portraits of Muslims are more harmful than the use of stereotypes of just about any other group, because Americans are unfamiliar with Islam and Muslims and yet quite familiar with other groups. As a result, Americans are unable to distinguish between what is reality and what is an over-amplification, exaggeration, or stereotype. With groups they are familiar with, Americans can distinguish stereotypes from fact. Until they are more familiar with the Muslim community, generalization disclaimers like the one Showtime ran before airing its original movie *Escape: Human Cargo* (1998), which portrayed many stereotypes of Muslims and Arabs, are useful and important and the responsibility of those who want to produce honest, realistic reports and works.

But even that is not enough—disclaimers should be shown throughout newscasts and productions that oversimplify Islam.

Clearly, American misunderstanding of Muslims is not unexpected or unreasonable considering the events that have occurred over the years, from the hostage crisis in Iran to the World Trade Center bombing. American Muslims' frustration mainly lies with media coverage of these events. Firstly, the media only reports the most sensational stories. Secondly, reporters tend to link Islam with the criminal act, as if to suggest that Muslims and Islam condone and approve of such criminal behavior.[6] When a Muslim does something bad, his religion is always noted by reporters. The same is rarely true for Christian and Jewish criminals, even if their religion motivated the act. Conversely, when a Muslim is behind a positive act, his religion is rarely reported in articles and reports on the event.

Third, the media packages information in ways that make Muslims look bad. News reports do not include the fact that Muslims in general condemn such events. Whether a Muslim is behind the act or not, mainstream Muslims are horrified by such acts. However, that point is not often raised by reporters. Suggestive headlines like "Terrorism Comes to America" and talk shows with themes like "Should We Americans Permit Muslims into the Country?" give all Muslims a negative image.[7] Talk shows are meant to be sensationalist and their message taken with a grain of salt; newspapers veer from their journalistic mission more subtly with intelligent-sounding titles that are actually unfairly anti-Islamic. Newspapers in particular use the word "fundamentalist" to signify Islam, grouping Islam with terrorists acts. The two words have become inseparable: "Islamic" is almost automatically followed by the term "fundamentalist."

In fact, no one has ever really defined what a Muslim fundamentalist is supposed to be and if the concept is legitimate or not, as there is no Arabic word for "fundamentalism." If there's no word in Arabic for fundamentalism, what does being a Muslim fundamentalist mean? Clearly the word is an "invention," as

Yvonne Haddad calls it, that suits media purposes.[8] We easily
define what we think Muslims are with this term and conclude
we don't need to learn anything else about Islam because the
term "Islamic fundamentalist" (or "Muslim fundamentalist")
sums up all that we have to say on the topic. Clearly the perpe-
trator in the World Trade Center bombing had sinister intent.
Is it fair to Muslims to equate this sinister intent with a strong
belief in Islam? Or fair to readers? What is to stop the average
New York Times reader from not making a distinction between
"fundamentalist" Islam and true Islam?

The primary *New York Times* article on the arrest of Moham-
med A. Salameh, eventually convicted of the World Trade Center
bombing, is relatively straightforward until the fourth paragraph, where writer Ralph Blumenthal abruptly introduces
Salameh's background as a so-called "Muslim fundamentalist."
He writes, "The arrest of Mr. Salameh, who law-enforcement
authorities say is a Muslim fundamentalist, provided the most
dramatic moment so far." He continues that the arrest "shifted
the focus from a wide array of possible suspects and motives . . .
onto a radical Islamic group that advocates violent revolution
against the Egyptian Government."[9] While the allegations of the
second sentence may be true, the mere phrase "Muslim fundamentalist" is the extent of the discussion on Islamic fundamentalism, *as if everyone already knows what that means,* and, therefore,
an explanation is unnecessary.

In its article on Salameh, the *Boston Globe* makes the same
mistake. The primary article, by Tom Mashberg, has a pointed
subtitle: "Man is held in N.Y. bombing: FBI, acting on clue from
van, seizes Muslim fundamentalist." Mashberg's *Globe* headline
is more damaging than its *New York Times* counterpart; it specifies that the suspect is a "Muslim fundamentalist," whatever
that may mean, in bold print at the very outset. The bombing and
the religion are thereby connected for all those who so much as
glance at the front page.

Mashberg seems obsessed with stereotyping Salameh. He
again points out that the suspect is a "Muslim fundamentalist" in
his lead sentence. In the third paragraph, Mashberg describes

Salameh as "thin and fidgety with a neat brown beard and heavy eyebrows." The article is continued on page 18, where the reader's eye is instantly drawn to a severe sketch of Salameh, a drawing that makes the Unabomber sketch look comforting. On this continued page, Mashberg writes about official investigation branching into "Muslim networks . . . in the New York area in what might turn out to be a broad terrorist presence in the nation."[10]

Mashberg's article is an example of the sensationalism writers used in reporting on the World Trade Center bombing. Why did he include such an eerie description of Salameh? His description of a beard and thick eyebrows just happens to fit many stereotypes of Arabs' appearance. Why run the haunting sketch of Salameh? Salameh appears dark and stiff in the foreground of a drawing that juxtaposes him against softly drawn and lighter-appearing attorneys and judge. It is as if the artist ground his pencil so hard in drawing Salameh that he ran out of lead for the attorneys and judge, causing then to look almost angelic with whiteness, particularly when compared to the dark presentation of Salameh.

Finally, Mashberg speculates about what "might" be an unprecedented terrorist regime in America. Though the important word is "might," a reader will have the impression that there *is* a terrorist network of Muslims in America. Such inattention to detail eventually causes us, the readers, to accept blindly unproven theories as facts: that all Muslim groups must have a chaos agenda. Readers will come away with the impression that terrorism is a way of life for Muslims and Muslim Arabs.

It is granted that there are Muslim terrorists and that the media is right to report on them. However, the media should establish a distinction between good Muslims and bad Muslims. Instead, newspapers and TV toss out the term "fundamentalist," say the suspect has a beard, and their job is done.

A few weeks later, the *New York Times* nearly redeemed itself by running a well-written article on Muslims protesting media coverage of the World Trade Center bombing.[11] I say "nearly" because this great article was buried on page 38! How many readers even saw it? The *New York Times*'s editors were smart to run the article in an obscure spot: they could take credit for paying attention to criticism, but they did not highlight media shortcomings and failures by printing the story anywhere where someone might actually notice.

Similarly, press coverage of the TWA Flight 800 crash on July 17, 1996, was also horrid. The major networks paraded out another legion of so-called experts—retired government officials and self-styled intellectuals—who pointed the finger at Muslims. Even without any evidence that the flight had crashed because of being attacked, Larry Johnson, a former State Department official, called it a "Pearl Harbor" with Muslims as the culprit. Newspaper headlines ceremoniously proclaimed Muslims as the prime suspects—an odd and far reaching conclusion since it was unclear that a crime had even been perpetrated. The media did everything to blame Muslims, according to CAIR, employing "overreaching labels," masking "sterotyping as analysis," and using unverified sources. The media did everything but report the facts.[12] Fame-seekers like and including Steve Emerson had another opportunity to enter our living rooms and minds and pass off their barely baked theories as expertise. What fools they made of us! Meanwhile, mechanical failure has been found to be the cause, and we indulged in stereotypes and fanciful stories of terrorist plot rings while the families of the victims were in agony.

Admittedly, radical Islamic extremists, called Islamists by academics, probably live in the United States, but their number must be small. According to FBI statistics, from 1980 until February 1996, only two of the 170 terrorist acts committed in the United States were carried out by radical Muslims.[13] However, there are not enough extremists among American Muslims to warrant alienating the entire group of four million people. The *Christian Science Monitor* says, "For now there is little evidence to show a growing Islamic conspiracy on U.S. shores, say official and unofficial sources."[14] In fact, the main reason anyone seems to think there may be a large number of American Muslim terrorists is because of the work of one journalist, Steven Emerson.

Emerson, though he relies on outdated speeches and lectures for evidence, manages in many prestigious newspaper articles and in his documentary, *Jihad in America,* to accuse mainstream Islamic groups of supporting Islamic terrorist movements. *Jihad,* which aired on PBS in November 1994, feebly attempts to prove that a large network of Muslim fundamentalist terrorists, and terrorist training and motivational conferences, exists in the United States. Emerson's work is well known as biased, anti-Islamic, and poorly researched. His agenda seems to be to create anti-Muslim hysteria, which he accomplished in the aftermath of the Oklahoma City bombing. But Emerson's mistakes in blaming Muslims, and there have been quite a few, have caused his credibility to be questioned.

In fact, coverage of the Oklahoma City bombing, which made Emerson infamous, is, in hindsight, well known to be American media's worst hour. Muslim stereotypes were used by the media and politicians. Muslims were immediately suspected by the public and by officials and, in some cases, pursued. The *Wall Street Journal,* one of the most respected American newspapers, was caught up in the anti-Islam hysteria after the bombing. The Islamic Society of North America (ISNA), the umbrella American Muslim organization which I personally know to be a mainstream group with no subversive activists in its history, held its Central Zone Conference in Tulsa, Oklahoma, two days before the bombing took place.[15] The day after the bombing, the *Wall Street Journal* reported that an Islamic fundamentalist group, referring to ISNA, held a meeting in Tulsa related to the bombing the weekend before it occurred—clearly an inaccurate report. Recently, the *Wall Street Journal* attacked the Democratic Party for having a Muslim perform the opening invocation at the 2000 convention on the basis that Muslims shouldn't be recognized.

The media continues to find new ways to discredit Islam. Currently, the topic du jour on maligning Islam is writing about the oppression of Muslim women. These reports are particularly annoying for a few reasons. First, the reporter rarely points out that patriarchal culture, not Islam, is to blame for such treatment. Second, the reporter, usually an American or Westerner, totally ignores similarly oppressive treatment in his or her own country.

Much blame for Muslims' negative image also lies with moviemakers, who seem to find it acceptable to attack Muslims. The release of the Disney film *Aladdin* (1992) was a watershed moment for Muslims and Arabs. Disney executives saw *Aladdin* as "simple entertainment" (as did moviegoers); but many Muslims and Arabs were offended by the vivid portrayal of anti-Muslim stereotypes.[16] Though it may seem ridiculous to attack *Aladdin,* stereotypes in films, like stereotypes in the news media, have consequences. Films may even leave a stronger impression on viewers than news media because films are free to make up whatever they want. (For a more detailed look at the films that have taken expansive creative liberties with portraying Islam, see the Close-Up accompanying this chapter.)

Where did these stereotypes come from? How did they become so popular? I believe that a combination of facts accounts for the existence of these stereotypes. First, the majority of Americans do not know much about Islam, its history, and its principles. Combine Americans' lack of knowledge with "the way we process information in America," that is with short snippets of news, highlights with few details, sound bites, and brief inflammatory statements, and one sees how those stereotypes can reign.[17] Those out to malign Islam, says prominent American Muslim Shahid Athar, "pick up one or two verses of the Qur'an and use it to express their own hatred of Islam and Muslims."[18] The absence of a prominent American-Muslim journalist to put images of Muslims and views of Islam into context allows Americans the opportunity to be frightened of Muslims.

Media treatment of Muslims causes potentially damaging stereotypes to persist. Virulent headlines have encouraged anti-Islamic views among Americans.[19] According to a nationwide poll conducted by the AMC, Islam has the highest unfavorable rating, 36 percent, and the lowest favorable rating, 23 percent, of any religious group in the survey, which included Roman Catholic, Presbyterian, Lutheran, Jewish, Fundamentalist Christian, Mormon, and Hindu.[20]

While Muslims were responsible for the Iranian hostage crisis and the World Trade Center bombing, those Muslims were not acting on behalf of all Muslims and were not, in all cases, American Muslims, yet media simplification causes us to hold all Muslims as responsible. The stereotypes hurt and affect all Muslims. The Council on American Islamic Relations (CAIR) says that in 1997, anti-Muslim incidents, such as vandalizing Islamic centers and assaulting individual Muslims, increased three-fold! In truth, American Muslims are more often victims of prejudiced acts or crimes than they are perpetrators of terrorism or prejudice themselves.

Many Muslims are verbally and physically harassed in America and receive hate mail, as my family does.[21] CAIR wrote a report in the summer of 1996, which followed the Oklahoma City bombing, chronicling 296 hate crimes directed at Muslims, mosques, and Islamic centers—296![22] Few have probably heard of the numerous attacks on mosques in recent years. Though the attacks are scattered and do not appear to form a pattern, they do suggest anti-Islamic feeling in America, particularly after the Oklahoma City bombing. A Muslim wasn't even responsible, but antagonism was incited. Furthermore, the same negative stereotypes that cause these crimes also result in the collective refusal (by non-Muslims) to label these actions as "hate crimes." People see vandalizing a mosque as a lesser offense than vandalizing a church or synagogue.

Pursuing the perpetrators of hate crimes is difficult for Muslims because many law enforcement officials seem to have learned what they know about Islam from the media. For example, American Muslims met with officials from the Federal Bureau of Investigation (FBI) in California to determine their level of knowledge about Islam and they were found to hold many stereotypes. Some FBI officials who attended the meeting mistakenly thought that Islamic ideology included an emphasis on violence.[23] As a result, how many crimes are overlooked because a Muslim is the victim? How many Constitutional guarantees are ignored because the suspect is Muslim?[24]

The negative stereotypes expounded in movies and the news plague American Muslims. Arab-American Khalid Diab, an engineer for a large company, was told at a party by an executive, "You aren't going to make vice president, and we both know why," implying Diab's heritage. "Ironically, while Diab's firm was glad to have him as a top scientist, it did not want him as a top manager." Diab, "[a]fter hearing Muslims were not responsible for the Oklahoma City bombing . . . asked: 'What if a Muslim did do it? What about the rest of us who never would? Why should we pay?'"[25]

In light of the misguided charges against Muslims during the Oklahoma City incident, "there . . . are signs of increased sensitivity to the interests of American Muslims," specifically their image.[26] A *USA Today* editorial printed at the time of the Oklahoma bombing emphasized that "Mainstream Islam preaches peace, and most Muslims are victims, not perpetrators, of terrorism."[27] Similarly, an incident in which two disc jockeys from KPBI radio station in Denver and a listener entered an Islamic Center in suburban Aurora and played the national anthem loudly, disturbing prayer services, was condemned by the station and amicably resolved. (The disc jockeys seemed to be acting in retaliation to Muslim and then Denver Nugget basketball player Mahmoud Abdul-Rauf's refusal to stand for the national anthem before games.) Part of the settlement included public apologies, to be aired on that station, as well as development of two important programs: an internship program for Muslims interested in the broadcasting industry and counseling programs for employees concentrating on awareness of and sensitivity to Muslims.[28]

A conference organized by the Rockefeller Foundation and CNN, held in Bellagi, Italy, in August 1996 addressed the subject, "Muslim images, Muslim realities in the American media."[29] Prominent American media executives, publishers, and broadcasters met with Islamic scholars, writers and educators "to discuss American media's perception of the Muslim world."

Western reporters are also being more critical of their fellow reporters, and the main improvement in negative stereotyping of Muslims has come from the media itself. Positive series and articles on American Muslims appearing in mainstream newspapers and magazines have been numerous in publications like the *New York Times* and the *Christian Science Monitor* as well as *U.S. News & World Report* and *Time*.[30] Local television affiliates and local newspapers are increasingly running positive stories on local Muslims.[31] These articles and reports originate from an intention different from exposing the acts behind a terrorist incident. The media seems to have a genuine and honest interest in and curiosity regarding American Muslims. I worry that these positive articles are sometimes patronizing, intentionally trying to make Islam look different. Hopefully, it's a step in the right direction.

Muslims have come a long way in media relations in the last few years. Media and law enforcement officials reached the nadir of negative stereotyping in instantly suspecting Muslims in the Oklahoma City bombing. Muslim Abraham Ahmed was detained as a suspect, and his family was harassed. Subsequently, as a reaction to their shortsightedness with Oklahoma, the collective media did not pin the Olympic Centennial Park bombing and subsequent ones on Muslims. In addition, the shooting of tourists at the Empire State Building in early 1997 was accurately reported, as opposed to exaggerated or sensationalized, despite the fact that a Muslim Palestinian is the known criminal. The fact that the shooter shot and killed himself at the end of the incident may be a mitigating factor; however, had this incident occurred only a few years earlier, it is not unreasonable to believe that the media would have reported the event in the same manner in which they reported on Oklahoma.

Most significant is the Central News Network's (CNN) 1998 live coverage of the annual pilgrimage to Mecca, or *hajj,* and a half-hour special report dedicated to the event. With two live updates every day throughout the pilgrimage, the coverage was unprecedented. CNN, and the CNN International Anchor, Riz Khan, set out to educate their world audience about Islam's beliefs and rituals. I think they succeeded and are to be commended for bringing a centuries-old tradition into the living rooms of families around the world. I think their coverage did more to dispel stereotypes than could have been imagined. In a similar vein, Muslims themselves are making more of an effort to show their friends and neighbors that they aren't set on blowing up buildings, by joining local groups and participating in multi-faith activities.

We have Muslim groups devoted to improving the image of Muslims to thank for events like Showtime's disclaimer. CAIR has worked very hard, as has the Muslim Public Affairs Council of California, whose main objective is to improve the public image of Muslims. In addition, the Islamic Networks Group of San Francisco, run by two Muslim women who are full-time volunteers and funded privately, conducts seminars and presentations on Islam for about 600 public and private school classes and 50 law enforcement training programs. The Council on Islamic Education (CIE) run by Shabbir Mansuri, and also out of California, works to correct textbooks' historical inaccuracies on Islam. Two organizations that focus on television are the Islamic Media Foundation, which has created public service announcements featuring NBA legend and Muslim Hakeem Olajuwan, and the Islamic Information Service (IIS). IIS has been a pioneer in the field, creating a weekly one-hour show about Islam for over the past ten years. The show, entitled "Islam," has aired on cable access all over the country. These Muslims work hard to show non-Muslim Americans an accurate view of Islam. They are truly doing us all a service by educating us.

If it is understood that the media will always scapegoat, can one say that the media has stopped using Muslims as a scapegoat? If the media bases such scapegoating on the world's political climate, then the answer to the above question is unknown. Single-cause journalists like Steven Emerson will probably still exist, but it is unlikely that they should dominate anymore. If the media, of its own volition, chooses alternately to blame and not blame Muslims, then American Muslims have a chance of escaping media scapegoating.

I would like to believe that the recent positive articles on Islam in America have helped to dispel widely circulated stereotypes and that the media is choosing to be more responsible. However, judging from the xenophobia the Islamic Saudi Academy faced, we can't be sure. I am counting on my fellow Americans to demand better journalism and to rise above misinformation.

CLOSE-UP
Movie Muslims: Myth versus Reality

My newest, latest favorite movie is Warner Brothers' *Three Kings* (1999). The movie is executed so creatively, mixing newsreel type footage of war scenes with interior shots of human anatomy. When I first heard *Three Kings* was about Desert Storm, I was sure it was the usual, stereotypical anti-Muslim fare. But I was totally wrong. Though the movie was about Desert Storm, the filmmakers went to great lengths to portray Arabs and Muslims as accurately as possible, hiring three Muslim consultants, who had the duty and ability to review the Arabic dialogue, props, sets, and costumes of the Arab characters as well as religious functions. A real story about the plight of the Iraqis after Desert Storm, this movie did what movies should: it moved me. For the first time, in a long time, Muslims were presented as real people in all their dimensions and not in stereotypes. One of the producers has often noted how much better *Three Kings* became because of the contribution of the Muslim consultants, giving the movie a more authentic and truer feel.

Not that Warner Brothers had a perfect record with Muslims. *Three Kings* was preceded by a nightmare of a movie. On one mild Saturday night, my friend Lara and I were surveying our movie choices and randomly decided to see Warner Brothers' *Executive Decision* (1996). The movie had just been released and looked like fun. Steven Seagal was prominently featured on the poster, so we expected a mindless action movie. What we actually saw was an egregiously offensive movie, with Steven Seagal's character promptly committing suicide, maybe sacrificially for the unsuspecting viewers.

Totally clueless about the plot, we sat patiently, awaiting the villains. Suddenly, talk of serving Allah and *jihad* amidst a suicide bombing and flying bullets was all over the movie! We both squirmed in our seats, uncomfortable with the blatant stereotypes. *Executive Decision* depicts actor Kurt Russell's attempt to rescue a plane headed for Washington, D.C., from Arab hijackers, who shoot and kill passengers without remorse while quoting Quranic passages and exclaiming Islamic phrases. The movie also shows the leader praying on the hijacked plane, as if to suggest that devout Muslims are violent. This image is equivalent to the juxtaposition of "Islamic" and "fundamentalism" in newspaper headlines: the two ideas become synonymous.

To make matters worse, the head Muslim terrorist announced that his name was Hasan—my own last name! It was like rubbing salt in my wounds. Not only were this character and I both Muslim, but we had the same name, too. That was where the similarities ended. I couldn't imagine anyone *more different* than I! Yet people who didn't know me and met me after seeing this movie would think of *Executive Decision*'s Hasan, regardless of how nice I was. Both Lara and I were upset about *Executive Decision*'s oversimplification of Islam and Muslims. In only one scene did another Muslim protest Hasan's reign of terror. This Muslim was promptly shot before his view could register with the audience.

One can presume that the makers of *Executive Decision* thought they were being accurate. It makes sense then that demands made by various American Muslim groups were not met; these groups, including CAIR, ISNA, and the Muslim Students' Association, asked that offensive portions be edited out of the movie before video release; that Warner Brothers publicly apologize to the Muslim community, and that Warner Brothers seek the advice of Muslims on any movie having to do with Muslims.[2] Such biased portrayals are damaging to Muslims like me, who would never think of hijacking planes. Islam is opposed to terrorism. In the Qur'an it is written, "If anyone killed a person not in retaliation of murder or for spreading mischief in the land it would be as if he killed all mankind" (5:32). Yet filmmakers don't seem to have an interest in making a film with at least one foot firmly based in reality. To Warner Brothers' credit, they chose to make *Three Kings* differently, with the advice of Muslims. The positive difference shows.

Jack Shaheen, an expert on popular depictions of Arabs and author of *The TV Arab,* says that negative stereotyping of Muslims and Arabs reached its apex in the years after Desert Storm, during which sixteen Hollywood films that ridicule Arabs had been made.[3] *True Lies* (1994), an Arnold Schwarzenegger movie that depicts an Islamic terrorist group, Crimson Jihad, has a charitable view of Arabs, presenting them as comically pathological and destructive (as opposed to just pathological and destructive). While *True Lies'* offenses are somewhat forgivable because the movie presented itself as a comedy, *Executive Decision* is more culpable because it took itself seriously.

The 1991 film *Not Without My Daughter* set Muslims back about ten years in the effort to improve their public image. The film is based on the book by American Betty Mahmoody, which chronicles the international abduction of her daughter by her Iranian father, Betty's husband, and her subsequent struggle to rescue her daughter. *Not Without My Daughter,* starring Sally Field, exemplifies stereotyping at its worst because, as professor of religion Margaret Miles writes in her book *Seeing and Believing: Religion and Values in the Movies:* "[O]ne woman's experience becomes the stereotype of a culture."[4] As is typical of the news media too, films tend to simplify Muslims—and present them only as one, large, awful, fundamentalist group. Few film critics bothered to review *Not Without My Daughter,* recognizing both its mediocrity and its racism, and "Those that did . . . agreed . . . it consisted of approximately 80 percent racism and 20 percent melodrama." Despite these poor reviews, *Not Without My Daughter* made fourteen million dollars when it first came out and, with no competing representation of Iranian Muslims and Islam, "enjoyed a monopoly in circulating its perspective on Islam and Muslims to a broad popular audience," the perspective that nice young American women are trapped into marriage with swarthy, hairy, foreign Muslim men who will eventually steal the couple's children.[5]

Miles says the obvious reason for making *Not Without My Daughter* in 1991 was Desert Storm. In addition, the film came out as the rapid growth of Islam in America was being noticed by the media and by Americans. Americans were curious about Muslims at home as well as abroad. *Not Without My Daughter* provided answers, but the wrong ones in my opinion.[6] The feeling one is left with after seeing the film is, at best, xenophobia and, at worst, the idea that Muslims are bad people with whom one should not associate. I do sympathize with women whose children have been abducted in a similar manner, but I don't think it's fair to characterize all of the Islamic community that way, which is the effect of the movie in the end.

More recently, a film made by *Glory* director Edward Zwick, *The Siege* (1998), is similarly flawed. Portraying Bruce Willis as an Army gereral who places New York under martial law and interns the male Muslim population of Brooklyn in a stadium, *The Siege* fails to drive in the point that such internment is wrong for any group of Americans because it violates and goes against American principles. I think the nuances that viewers are supposed to glean from the movie may be lost on many. While intellectual lightweights defend the movie as expressing an inconceivable prospect (internment of Muslims and Arabs), specifically Martin Peretz, in the *New Republic*, I point them to our country's use of Secret Evidence. Currently, the Immigration and Naturalization Service (I.N.S.) is holding about twenty immigrant Muslims or Arabs in I.N.S. detention centers.[7] Those detained legal residents, have not been allowed to see the evidence they are being held on, on the basis that revealing such evidence would threaten national security. (In those cases where the evidence has been finally revealed, the evidence in fact did not contain any information important to national security.) As a result, those held cannot defend themselves. Why is it that only Arabs and Muslims are being held (or "interned" as *The Siege* put it)? Though some say that Muslims are merely the new enemy "du jour," there is no denying that movies like *The Siege* visually connect Islamic religious acts like prayer with terrorism.[8] I think the makers of *The Siege* tried to express a connection between CIA guerilla training and Islamic terrorism, but, in the end, the Muslims are still the bad guy.

Disney wins the Steve Emerson award for employing and popularizing as many stereotypes as possible. Over the span of a few years, Disney has made a number of anti-Islam movies. Richard Scheinin lists the offenses of Disney's *Aladdin* (1992): "characters are portrayed as grotesque, with huge noses and sin-

ister eyes . . . violent" characteristics reflective of "the negative
stereotyping with which Hollywood and the media have
stamped Arabs and Muslims for nearly a century."[9] Besides
irrevocably changing the meaning of the original Arabic story,
probably changing many positive Islamic aspects of the story,
Disney painted a portrait of Arabs that showed them as belligerent. The lyrics to the opening song of *Aladdin*, "Arabian Nights,"
included lines about how the character is from a barbaric place
where "they cut off your ear if they don't like your face."

Though Disney eventually gave in to American Muslim
groups' pressure and softened the effect of some lyrics in the
home video, most fans know them in their racist and anti-Islam
form.[10] Despite the clear prejudice of such lines, we continue
to love Disney. Songs from *Aladdin* are popularly used in
children's music classes.[11] The Academy of Motion Picture Arts
and Sciences honored *Aladdin* with two Academy Awards,
American filmmaking's highest honor.

In spite of all the time American Muslim groups invested in
educating Disney executives after the release of *Aladdin*, Disney
made similar mistakes with *The Return of Jafar* (1994), a
straight-to-video-release sequel to *Aladdin*. Hardly two years
after Disney corrected some of *Aladdin*'s stereotypes, *The Return of
Jafar*, in Jack Shaheen's estimation, "displayed gobs of hook-nosed
Arabs referred to in the film as 'desert skunks.'" Disney sold ten
million copies of *The Return of Jafar*, making it one of the best-
selling videos of all time. Disney's 1995 Christmas season movie,
Father of the Bride, Part II, portrays an excessively wealthy
Arab couple, the Habibs. Mr. Habib, fittingly thick-accented and
bearded, cons the main character out of $100,000.[12] Disney
employs such stereotypes in other movies and products as well.

Furthermore, Disney, from an executive level, does not seem
interested in resolving differences with Arabs and Muslims.
Meanwhile, they have a compelling hold over the minds and
hearts of children (and pocketbooks of parents). Shaheen says
that he and many others, including Muslim American groups,
wished to talk with Disney executives Michael Eisner, Michael
Ovitz, and Joe Roth about stereotypes in Disney's film *Kazaam*

(1996). Those groups and Shaheen have yet to hear from anyone at Disney. As a result of the executives' indifference, the American-Arab Anti-Discrimination Committee, in conjunction with other groups concerned about negative stereotyping, organized nationwide protests in August, 1996. Shaheen feels that no Muslims or Arabs with clout are involved in the film industry; as a result of Muslim Americans' "[b]eing invisible," Disney can take as many liberties in depicting Muslim Americans as they like.[13]

What is most troublesome about media representation of Muslims is not that newspaper publishers and film executives allow inaccurate portrayals to dominate; their overall goal is to make money, either by selling newspapers or tickets, however sensational. What is shameful is how prominent journalists and actors have contributed to perpetuating stereotypes. Journalists are supposed to be committed to the truth and actors to achieving artistry. Where is the truth or artistry in demonizing Muslims and simplifying and generalizing Islam? Respectable journalists like A. M. Rosenthal of the *New York Times* and prominent actors like Sally Field, people who influence Americans, not only allowed negative stereotypes of Muslims to exist but made them worse.

Fortunately for them, these stereotypes are so entrenched that they do not have to worry about being condemned for their insensitivity. Similar portrayals of Jews, Africans, Hispanics, the elderly, children, students—practically every other group of Americans—would not be tolerated. Edward Said says in his book, *Covering Islam,* "Malicious generalizations about Islam have become the last acceptable form of denigration of foreign culture in the West." Ironically, prominent Hollywood actors are speaking out against Germany's treatment of Christian Scientologists and Germany's banning of films starring actors who follow Christian Scientology.[14] Hollywood's representation of Muslims is no fairer than Germany's treatment of Christian Scientologists; in fact, Hollywood may be more to blame because they do not even realize their offenses.

Believing inaccurate depictions of Muslims, both in movies and in the media, to be harmless is a dangerous view. Movies and images have consequences. Shaheen cites how "[g]rotesque stereotypes . . . [c]ontinuously repeated . . . engender harm." Movies with anti-Semitic themes made during the Third Reich partially led to the Holocaust. Pre–World War II Hollywood movies satirizing the Japanese played a role in the internment of Japanese-Americans.[15] Margaret Miles similarly recognizes that *Not Without My Daughter* came down strongly against Muslims and pro-fear and hatred.[16] With movies and in the news media, the acts of a group of Muslims or one Muslim has meant the condemnation of all Muslims. We pay the price for these stereotypes everyday: when attendants refuse to serve us because we wear the headcover, or *hijab;* when we're taken aside at airports for questioning, followed around stores and our every move watched by clerks; when our places of worship are vandalized; when we are turned away from jobs because of a "foreign look"; when we receive threatening unsigned letters; when other Muslims we know are physically assaulted; and when the children of our community are called "camel jockey" and "desert rat" at school.

Islamic vigilance and criticism has paid off in some instances, such as with African-American director Spike Lee's *Malcolm X* (1992). Lee's movie was the first major Hollywood movie in contemporary cinema to deal with Islam in a meaningful way and portray Islam accurately. The scenes of the pilgrimage to Mecca, known as *hajj,* in particular are evocative of Islamic principles as Malcolm shares his religious experience with Muslims of all races and backgrounds. Overall though, the stereotypes persist. When Muslims see themselves accurately portrayed in a movie, they are overjoyed. When Muslim Mary Lahaj went to see *Al-rasul* or *The Message* (1976), she was converted to Islam again, identifying with the pain of the struggle the movie depicted. Realizing how much she didn't know, she embarked upon a path to learn her religion. American Muslims also enjoyed *Robin Hood: Prince of Thieves* (1990), starring Kevin Costner. The portrayal of Robin's African slave, played by Morgan Freeman, was fair and, actually, moving for Muslims. As Muslims speak out against inaccurate portrayals of Muslims, they celebrate and recognize those movies that are responsibly done.

The English Patient, a financially and critically successful movie released in 1996 by Miramax Pictures, has several Muslim characters in small roles who are portrayed, for the most part, positively.

Director Renny Harlin's *The Long Kiss Goodnight* (1996) has a clever plot twist that plays on the American media's rush to stereotype Muslims and Arabs. In addition to great action and acting, the plot is fascinating. The CIA, in an effort to gain additional funding from Congress, hires an ex-CIA operative to stage a bombing on the U.S.-Canada border. The catch is that the former operative is going to make the bombing look like a real terrorist attack by planting the body of a dead Arab man at the site. The CIA and its former operative feel safe in assuming that once the body is discovered the American media will finish their job for them, by blaming Muslim terrorists. The American public and Congress will agree with the media, too. No investigation will take place, and Congress will gladly increase the CIA's budget, so as to prevent more international terrorism on domestic land. The movie's heroine and hero eventually foil the CIA and the operative before their plan can take effect.

I find this plot point ingenious! Harlin is an innovative, creative filmmaker for presenting another set of "bad guys" whose motives are so sinister that they play on Americans' preset fears and stereotypes. *The Long Kiss Goodnight* points out that Americans have already bought into the stereotype of Muslims as terrorists, whether they really are or not.

More recently, *Air Force One* (1997), starring Harrison Ford, could easily have become another *Executive Decision.* For some reason, the writer chose to make the terrorists hijacking the President's plane Russian. Though revisiting enemies of the Cold War in our movies may not seem like progress, I have come to appreciate films like *Air Force One* that choose not to oversimplify issues and resort to Islam as a quick and easy enemy-depiction. In fairness, Russians suffered a lot of negative portrayals as Communists throughout the Cold War era. However,

Air Force One draws a distinction between Russian terrorists and regular Russians and is not gratuitous in its portrayal of Russian terrorists as villains. One does not walk away thinking, "That is all I know about Russians." I think Hollywood is trying to be more creative with its villains, too, as the Arab terrorist stereotype may have grown old, finally. The James Bond movie *Tomorrow Never Dies* (1997) has a media mogul, a la Rupert Murdoch, as its villain.

Perhaps most heartening is cable channel Showtime's reaction to criticism by American Islamic groups and American Muslims about its original movie, *Escape: Human Cargo* (1998), based on a book by an American businessman who effectively was trapped in Saudi Arabia once his passport was taken away by his employer. Despite the fact that the movie was a critical bomb, Muslims nonetheless objected to the negative portrayal of Arabs and Islam, worrying that viewers would see all Muslims as belligerent and warped. About a year earlier, Muslims had unsuccessfully lobbied Home Box Office (HBO) to prevent viewers from generalizing about all Muslims after watching *Path to Paradise* (1997), its original movie depicting events surrounding the World Trade Center bombing. They had much more luck with Showtime, which deserves credit for running a disclaimer before the airing of *Escape: Human Cargo:* "This is one person's experiences and does not reflect Arab culture or the Islamic faith." Though I think the disclaimer should have been run throughout the movie, the mere fact that Showtime decided to run one is a slam-dunk for American Muslims working to improve the public image of Muslims and Islam.

We, Muslims, as an American community, have to work together to bring an end to harmful stereotypes. It is the job of Arabs and Muslims to educate our fellow Americans about our religion and culture. It is the job of our fellow Americans to listen to our criticisms with an open mind. Together we can become a more educated audience, with low tolerance for poor filmmaking that relies on stereotypes to make up for a film's flaws.

── 6 ◆ American Muslim Women: Between Two Worlds ──────

I was debating with my extended family once during a family gathering whether Muslim women and men should be allowed to pray in the same room. I reasoned that on Judgment Day men and women will stand equally before God with no gender preference. My grandfather piped up, "No, men are superior in Islam!" We were in my uncle's normally quite noisy Suburban, which had now gone silent at my grandfather's words.

My family members waited a moment, and then said things like, "Oh no!" and "You're in for it now, grandfather!" They were saying all this because I am known in my family for responding vehemently to such statements. I stayed levelheaded, however, and asked my grandfather, "You mean in the Qur'an?"

"Yes!" he said.

"I don't think so," I said.

"No, it says it!" he retorted.

After a few minutes of this yes-no business we finally got to the merits of the argument. My grandfather felt that since God's messengers were all male, men must then be superior in God's eyes. I countered that a woman, Khadijah, Muhammad's wife, was the first convert to Islam. Without her faith in Muhammad, *no Muslims would exist.*

I offered other arguments proving gender equality in Islam, but something told me that my points were falling on deaf ears. I joked that my grandfather must have received the Taliban version of the Qur'an. The Taliban are the Islamic revolutionaries who took over the Afghanistan government and banned women from working because they said that was against their interpretations of the Qur'an. The country came to a near stand-still as half the professional population—doctors, teachers—were not allowed to work. Obviously, the Taliban had to modify some of their policies to keep the country functioning. The Talikan validly has pronounced that they put an end to Afghanistani tribal practices which hurt women. They were forced to marry and had no right to property or divorce. So as unenlightened as the Taliban is, they have actually elevated Afghanistan's rural population.

Though I tried to make light of the situation, I was saddened that *my own grandfather* would say such a thing, even if he believed it. Does he really think that I, as a woman, am inferior to my brother, merely because he's male? I see in my grandfather the effects of South Asian culture, which is patriarchal, on his interpretation of the Qur'an. Sure, there are a few passages that taken out of context, interpreted from a patriarchal perspective, or not updated for our times (which the Qur'an instructs us to do) imply women's inferiority. They are by no means passages on which to build tenets of Islam, however. When I asked my grandfather to show me where in the Qur'an it says that women are inferior to men, he replied that it would take him some time to find the passage. As he has still not found it, I presume it doesn't exist or isn't clear in its meaning.

But this is what it came to—my own grandfather, a product of his society and prejudices, saying that women are inferior to men. This despite the fact that women outnumber men in his own family. He has five granddaughters and three grandsons— it's in his interest to see women as equal to men! It hurts, but I understand that we all have to read the Qur'an and make our own interpretation. This is my *jihad* with my grandfather. Who knows—maybe someday my grandkids will disagree with me on a belief, emphasized by my American culture, on something similar.

The debate over the status of women in Islam is probably the best example of how culture affects interpretation. Men like my grandfather have taken a few Qur'anic passages and, coupled with a patriarchal culture, have interpreted them in the most literal and self-serving way. It happens in all cultures, not just among Muslims, and such chauvinism existed before Islam, perhaps even before organized religion itself. There is no Islamic basis for demeaning women or oppressing them. Culture is the culprit here, and no one really is immune from that.

American culture often favors men and holds women back. Women are paid less than men for similar jobs. We have yet to elect a female president. We're still arguing over a woman's right to control her body. Sexual harassment and rape are very difficult to prosecute. Office politics, sometimes on a subliminal level, keep women from rising to top positions. However, no one sees the American woman as being as severely oppressed as the Muslim woman. Women *are* oppressed in *some* countries where the majority of the population is Muslim. There, women's literacy rates are often quite low, among many other disadvantages for advancement.

However, such oppression is not mandated by the Qur'an. It is in fact condemned by it. Furthermore, strong Muslim women are all over the place. Benazir Bhutto became the prime minister of Pakistan twice, which is more than we can say for a female politician in the United States. Muhammad's wife Khadijah, was one of the most successful business people in Mecca. Fatima Mernissi is one of the most intelligent Islamic scholars and a prominent thinker, and she is a woman. My own mother runs the lives of our family as well as being a dynamic volunteer worker and fundraiser. My dad calls her "the boss" and sometimes a tyrant. Here I am writing a book on Islam in America. Do I seem oppressed to you?

The challenge women like my mom and I face is to overcome the cultural baggage that haunts American Muslim women. Though women in Islamic countries are often oppressed, Islam as a philosophy is very pro-woman. However, as with all philosophies, societies, and cultures, contradictions occur in the journey from paper (Qur'an) to practice (my grandfather). Because of these contradictions, Muslim women all over the world are being pulled in two different directions: one is to fulfill the traditional expectations for a Muslim woman, like marriage at a young age and raising a family; the other to explore the new roles for women in the modern world by being career women and community activists.

The problems we face—in trying to express our feminism, become activists, and be independent—are acute versions of what American women in general are going through. As more American women convert to Islam and more young Muslim women like me grow up, it is in our interest, as Americans, not to be like my grandfather and rely on what we have heard through the grapevine, but to encourage all women to explore their identities and their strengths, and instill in them the belief that they can contribute to our society, our economy, our values as much as men can.

Who is the American-Muslim woman? The Islamic Council of New England Conference (ICNE) on "Women in Islam" said all Muslim women should be knowledgeable about Islam and become mothers.[1] Women are also expected to be modest and keep interaction with males to a minimum, making activities outside the home difficult.[2] According to Aminah McCloud, these aspects associated with the term "Muslim woman" arrived upon the American scene with Muslim immigrants in the later part of the twentieth century; these immigrant Muslim women wore strict Islamic dress and were committed to raising children as well as being obedient to their husbands.[3]

These traditional views are not the only choices, however. Jane Smith, a scholar on Islam, presents a more open view in her essay "Islam" in the book *Women in World Religions:* "The new Islamic woman . . . is morally and religiously conservative and affirms the absolute value of the true Islamic system for human relationships." This new Muslim woman disagrees with an interpretation of Islam that oppresses women. She is quite open to educational and professional advancement for herself, though she may think some professions are more appropriate for women than others. Additionally, she does not mind extending sole decision-making power to a male member of her family in certain circumstances in return for security.[4]

In reality, today's American Muslim female community is a mix of all these models: educated and uneducated, married and unmarried, liberal and conservative, as diverse a population as American women in general. For example, I am educated, do not wear *hijab,* expect to have a career, a good marriage (possibly arranged), and kids. You're probably thinking that those expectations are not all that different from those of the average American woman, with the exception of the *hijab* and arranged marriage.

For many Muslim girls, arranged marriage or semi-arranged to someone your parents introduced to you is no more odd than dating and marrying one of your older brother's friends, or someone you met at work. The same is true of *hijab.* Muslims have been exposed to these traditional aspects of Islam for most of their lives.

American Muslim women are really between two worlds: the old world of traditions, preserved and passed down by immigrant parents or older members of the indigenous community, and the new world, as presented to us by the feminist movement, American emphasis on gender equality, and by the Qur'an, in a sense, too.

The idea of a Muslim feminist strikes Americans as odd. American Muslim women are in the unique and paradoxical position of living in a society where they are free to explore their religion but are stereotyped by the greater population of their country as oppressed. The West cites its perceptions of arranged marriages, polygamy (actually polygyny, meaning a plurality of wives), veiling, and other aspects of Islamic life that are perceived to degrade women as evidence of Islam's cultural inferiority.[5]

At the same time as they encounter this criticism, American Muslim women are rediscovering the freedoms Islam gives them.

Muslims believe that God revealed to Prophet Muhammad several provisions emphasizing a woman's independence, provisions which are recorded in the Qur'an. Of particular note is that in the Qur'an Eve is created independently of Adam, providing no Qur'anic basis for women's existence as the result of the creation of men.

In the Qur'an, men and women are fully equal before God. Marriage is a contract to be negotiated, even to the woman's benefit, and women have the right to divorce, one of many Qur'anic "innovations" that "brought legal advantages for women quite unknown in corresponding areas of the Western Christian world," says Jane Smith.[6] Other innovations include the right to own property and the right to inherit money.[7] According to Islamic law, a woman can keep her maiden name and her personal income. Islam also grants women the right to participate in political affairs and vote (imagine, if we had all followed the Qur'an, there would have been no need for the suffragette movement), to stand equally with men in the eyes of the law, to receive child support in the event of a divorce, to seek employment and education, to accept or turn down a marriage proposal, and to live free from spousal abuse.[8] Islam also gives women high status as mothers, to be respected and admired by their children. On two occasions the Prophet highlighted the mother's role, telling one follower to stay with his mother rather than join the military, "for Paradise is at her feet."[9] Muslim women also can draw on a history of strong women, particularly those who lived in Muhammad's time.[10] Some Muslims even support a woman's right to abortion because the procedure is believed to have been performed in the Prophet's time without his dissent.[11]

However, along with Qur'anic tradition, one is also subject to other traditions that, over centuries, have come to be associated with being Muslim, though they may have nothing to do with Islam, like female circumcision (a custom pre-dating both Islam and Christianity found along the Nile River, deep into Africa)

and an emphasis on marriage. Furthermore, women bear the brunt of traditional aspects of cultures associated with Islam—like wearing *hijab*. Algerian lawyer and specialist in Muslim women's rights for UNESCO, Wassyla Tamzali, told the *New York Times,* "[W]omen symbolize tradition and cultural identity. It is as if the whole burden of the Islamic tradition rests on their shoulders."[12] Rifaat Hassan, an American Muslim scholar, writes, "Even when a Muslim woman is able to acquire an education and secure a job, she is seldom able to free herself from the burden of traditionalism that confronts her on all sides."[13]

This coercive nature of traditional aspects of Islam manifests itself in America with an emphasis on marriage, in my opinion. Young Muslim women are bombarded with messages not only about the importance of marriage but of marriage *at a young age.* Even with parents and families like mine, who show hardly any vestiges of traditionalism or conservatism (grandfathers notwithstanding), the pressure for daughters to marry young is strong. That is a part of American-Muslim culture, for better or for worse. But I'd be lying if I said I didn't feel pressured to marry soon by my community. There doesn't seem to be a really good reason to do so, other than that marriage in our culture is a preferred alternative to dating, as sex outside of marriage is *haram* (unlawful). Marriage at a young age or marriage at all is not a religious obligation, but the centrality of family in Islamic culture makes marriage very important. In addition, marriage means acceptance into the Muslim social community. For example, Carol Anway, who surveyed American women who converted to Islam and wrote *Daughters of Another Path: Experiences of American Women Choosing Islam,* found that unmarried respondents sometimes felt uncomfortable among other Muslims because they were not married.[14]

The importance of marriage in the American Muslim community is exemplified by the myriad ways the community has developed for finding a spouse: personal advertisements in Islamic publications, matrimonial booths at Islamic conferences, enlisting peers in a search or through "word of mouth" and mosque-arranged singles gatherings.[15] American Islamic publications run how-to articles on finding a spouse. Marriage is so important that immigrant parents worry about a scarcity of young Muslim men for their daughters; some even wonder if the Islamic law allowing Muslim men to marry Christian or Jewish women should be rescinded in America.[16]

In many ways, it's good that the community is taking an active role in pairing off young people. As a result of parental flexibility and the perception of a scarcity of Muslims of similar ages, inter-ethnic marriages have become more popular, particularly intermarriage between racial backgrounds. That sounds like the American dream to me: young married people, sometimes of diverse backgrounds, with a stable financial footing and strong family setting.

A more subtle form of oppression against American Muslim women is carried out by American Muslim men who feel threatened by modern American culture. Rifaat Hassan writes, "Nothing perhaps illustrates men's deep insecurities . . . so well as the sternness and strictness with which they compel their women to cover themselves from head to foot and keep them confined to their houses."[17] Kathleen Gough, in her essay, "The Origin of the Family," says that one of the characteristics of male power is physical confinement and prevention of movement of women; this characteristic is manifested by *purdah* (the separation of men and women at all gatherings especially during prayer, which has no solid Qur'anic basis but is practiced by most Muslims) and *hijab*.[18] Muslim men, and eventually the females in their community, force *hijab* and severe forms of modesty on women that result in gender segregation.[19] Such behavior is sometimes coerced onto Muslim women through community attitudes and chalked up to the noble purpose of protecting women. These attitudes are reminiscent of how the Christian male group, the Promisekeepers, allegedly protects its women. With both groups, a fine line exists between protection and encouragement versus oppression and suppression.

Enforcing certain standards of behavior on the women of the community probably confirms the worthiness of their efforts to live as Muslims in America (or as Promisekeepers), as if to show visibly that they are succeeding. Some efforts at protecting American Muslim women originate from genuine worries; most do not. Louis Farrakhan seems sincere in *A Torchlight for America:*

> There are sanctuaries for birds. There are seasons when you can't hunt certain animals. But it's open season on women all the time. Women are constantly bombarded by sexual advances and negative messages so much so that they are often put into vulnerable positions that bring evil consequences.[20]

His sentiment is admirable and speaks to a woman embattled by emphasis on her appearance and sexual harassment at the workplace. However, most male protective efforts seem motivated by paranoid feelings and result in restricting women's activities. A *Muslim Journal* article quotes a prominent African-American Muslim man as saying,

> These non-Muslims love Muslim girls. . . . It is no secret that the young Muslim girls are virgins and they are chaste and look beautiful. So we are victimized and subjected to that kind of pressure and tension. . . . And it is becoming increasingly more difficult to deal with that in this society.[21]

His words show how he, and probably others, see the preservation of Muslim girls' chastity as a barometer of their success as American Muslims. As a result, women are often pressured by their communities to be and act a certain way.

Many Muslim women consent to their own subjugation because they believe "boys will be boys." A female kindergarten teacher in her mid-twenties said in an interview, "Many people think we're [NOI and Muslim women] covered just to hide our bodies, but the main reason is that men are still in the beast stage."[22] A parent of one of the converts surveyed by Carol Anway responds, "I feel like Islamic men are so afraid of their sexuality that the women have the burden of helping them control it."[23] I'm not sure that American Muslim men necessarily have American Muslim women's best interests at heart. It should be up to women to decide how they will conduct themselves.

Though the problems Muslim women face seem insurmountable, women can improve their situation by taking advantage of the opportunities a Muslim woman has in America. Living in the United States is positively affecting the lives of American Muslim women in two ways: (1) American culture encourages female participation in religious activities; and (2) Muslim women are readily able to learn Arabic, read the Qur'an, and analyze the Qur'an for themselves.

One of the greatest phenomena occurring in the Muslim world today is Qur'anic exegesis by Muslim feminists. The Qur'an, a book regarded as the divine word for over 1400 years, is being interpreted from a non-male perspective on a large scale for *the first time ever*. A diverse group of the world's female Muslims are "fundamentally rework[ing Islam] . . . from a feminist and egalitarian point of view."[24] Their work is controversial because they are trying to prove that the Qur'an does not support oppression of women without undermining or questioning the validity of the Qur'an itself, only certain interpretations. Some credit the Beijing United Nations Conference on women for bringing this intellectual, yet politically charged, dialogue to the surface, and now the Ford Foundation, the National Endowment for Democracy, and the Council on Foreign Relations are funding projects in this area.[25]

I say it's about time. For 1400 years, men like my grandfather have told women like me what the Qur'an says. I'm not saying all those men are wrong. And frankly, the only interpretations I'm really interested in challenging are the ones regarding women's so-called inferiority. I'm just saying that, now that women have an opportunity to be literate, to read the Qur'an in Arabic, and tell us if they think God made men superior, let's have a listen!

The core complaint of these feminist Muslim theologians is that though the Qur'an is clear in its support of women's rights, men have been interpreting the Qur'an to their own advantage since its revelation. Amina Wadud-Muhsin, philosophy and religion professor at Virginia Commonwealth University in Richmond, says, "[N]ow . . . many women are making the point that . . . men's interpretation of our religion . . . has limited women's progress, not our religion itself." For example, the gender segregation during prayer now suggests inferiority on women's part when, in actuality, the Prophet initiated the practice so that women would not have to prostrate in front of men.[26] Realizing that a male perception of Islam has been used and accepted for centuries, Muslim women are taking back their right to Qur'anic education and interpretation.

The movement is part of an Islamic renaissance worldwide that gives Muslim women the opportunity to study Islam. Critics of the movement, orthodox and mainstream Muslims, claim that it is yet another tactic to discredit Islam. But Muslim theologian and religion professor Rifaat Hassan at the University of Louisville believes that "What we are witnessing today is the beginning of one of Islam's greatest revolutions, the women's revolution." Feminist scholars like Hassan feel they are strengthening Islam against the standard Western criticisms of female oppression.[27]

For example, American Muslim men are trying their best to explain *Surah* [Qur'anic chapter] 2:228 and 4:34, passages emphasizing men's superiority. The dominant translation of 4:34, one handed down over centuries, advocates hitting one's wife *lightly* in *extreme* cases.[28] A. J. Arberry's translation reads, "And those you fear may be rebellious admonish; banish them to their couches, and beat them."[29] Kamran Memon says of this troublesome passage in his article "Wife Abuse in the Muslim Community":

Tragically, some Muslim men actually use Islam to "justify" their abusive behavior. Focusing on rituals, considering themselves to be Islamically knowledgeable, and disregarding the spirit of Islam, they wrongly use the Qur'anic verse that says men are the protectors and maintainers of women to go on power trips, demand total obedience, and order their wives around. They disregard the Islamic requirement for the head of the household to consult with other members of the family when making decisions. Then, if their wives dare to speak up or question their orders, these men misinterpret a Qur'anic verse that talks about how to treat a disobedient wife and use it as a license for abuse.[30]

Muslim women are reinterpreting the texts for themselves and pointing out alternate, less controversial, and possibly more accurate interpretations. The usual explanation, which Memon cites, of the more offensive translation (including the instructions to beat) is that men, in Islam, have the large burden of keeping their houses in order and must carry out their responsibilities as they see fit.[31] Hassan's analysis gives a different perspective:

> The first point to be noted is that it [the Qur'anic passage that is interpreted to advocate beating] is addressed to *ar-rijal* ("the men") and to *an-nisaa* ("the women"). In other words, it is addressed to all men and women of the Islamic community. . . . Here, it is important to point out that the Arabic word that is generally translated as "beating," when used in a legal context as it is here, means "holding in confinement," according to the authoritative lexicon *Taj al-'Arus*. . . . I have analyzed sura 4, verse 34 in order to show how the words of the Qur'an have been mistranslated in order to make men the masters and women the slaves.[32]

Though not all American Muslim women can be scholars like Hassan, they can benefit from the American tradition of women participating in church activities every Sunday. Women participate in and run fundraising activities, and they attend the Sunday service as well as teach Sunday School.

American ideals have influenced Islamic religious practice in those two ways: women are recognized as suitable teachers, and activities are held on the American holy day, Sunday. Immigrant women's participation in the mosque is definitely greater in the United States than in most of the Islamic world.

For both immigrants and American-born women, participating in mosque activities can be empowering when they take the opportunity. If it weren't for American culture that emphasized Sundays as a gathering day for everyone in the family, American Muslim women might never have gained leadership roles in the mosque. In this case, American culture has trumped chauvinistic immigrant culture.

Just as they're not waiting for men to start translating the Qur'an for them, Muslim women are also not waiting for men to solve community problems that affect Muslim women, specifically by opening women's shelters. The shelters exemplify what American Muslim women can achieve when they work together and how American Muslim women *can positively affect American society.* These shelters are needed; M. Riaz Khan writes in *Islamic Horizons:* "The number of instances of domestic violence in many Muslim communities is steadily rising."[33] Memon writes, "Based on information from Muslim leaders, social workers, and activists in North America, the North American Council for Muslim Women says that approximately 10 percent of Muslim women are abused emotionally, physically, and sexually by their Muslim husbands."[34]

Two women's shelters in the United States cater to Muslim women, *Apna Ghar* in Chicago and the *Niswa* shelter in Torrance, California. Because they receive government funds, they are both open to all needy women. The two shelters also are financed by private donations. *Apna Ghar,* which means "our house" in Hindi, is the older of the two, and "is the result of cooperative efforts initiated by Asian ethnic minority and immigrant communities," including Muslims of South Asian descent. Its primary goal is to house temporarily women and children seeking shelter from domestic violence in order to "enhance their sense of dignity and self respect." Responding to reports of increasing violence in Asian-American households, *Apna Ghar* opened in 1989, the first shelter of its kind. Highlights of the services provided from July 1996 to June 1997 are 368 hours of advocacy on issues ranging from housing and literacy to child care, 2,668 hours of counseling, handling of 1,344 hotline calls, assistance in obtaining jobs for 133 individuals, 754 hours of legal advocacy, and providing shelter for 136 women and children, among other services.[35]

The second shelter is run by an organization called *Niswa,* which stands for the National Islamic Society of Women of America, a group founded in 1990 that "seeks to provide aid to needy Muslim families, single mothers and children, and victims of war and other disasters."[36] The name also means "women" in Arabic. In September 1996, *Niswa* opened the Amina Adaya shelter, named after its benefactor, for women victimized by domestic abuse. "Niswa is uniquely equipped to serve those . . . of Middle Eastern and South Asian background, with special cultural and language needs." The *Niswa* shelter offers services similar to *Apna Ghar*'s: a 24-hour hotline, counseling, legal advocacy, and services for children, among others.[37] Recently, *Niswa* began handling adoptions, placing Muslim children with Muslim families.

The women who founded and run these shelters are impressive and an example for all Muslims to follow. Shahmim Ibrahim, a Muslim of South Asian descent, founded *Niswa.* She emigrated to the United States in the 1970s and is a trained psychotherapist. She says,

> [T]here were no social service organizations in our community here. There were many, many mosques. . . . Their hands are full with lectures, weddings, *Juma* [Friday] prayers . . . we needed this organization so we can meet the social welfare needs of the community. . . . I got two or three women together, and I told them about the idea, that it's about time that we did something.

After becoming incorporated as a non-profit organization, their workload increased, defining their activities: "We never dreamed when we formed that we would be opening a shelter. . . . [T]he needs kept arising."[38]

Ibrahim's counterpart at *Apna Ghar,* Najma Adam, has a similarly activist attitude. Like Ibrahim, the executive director of *Apna Ghar* at the time of my research is of South Asian descent and Muslim; she was born in Uganda, however, and moved to the United States as a young child. She has a master of arts degree in Social Service Administration from the University of Chicago and, since I conducted my research, has left *Apna Ghar* to seek full-time a doctorate from the Jane Addams School of Social Work at the University of Illinois at Chicago. She worries about how a Muslim woman's accusations of abuse are downplayed in the Islamic community by male religious leaders:

> Islam does not say . . . use force. . . . [W]hen . . . [a] woman sits in my office . . . crying . . . and she's got scars everywhere to show for [the abuse] . . . I . . . want to . . . say . . . [w]here in the Qur'an does it [advocate abuse]? A man should not do that and . . . religious figures will always be biased . . . towards the man.[39]

Adam's assessment is serious and definitely controversial in the American Muslim and Islamic world. The abuse, however, appears to be indisputable and must be dealt with.

Memon agrees with Adam that the abuse is often overlooked, especially verbal abuse:

> Although it's completely contrary to the example of Prophet Muhammad, peace be upon him, the Muslim community nonetheless tends to dismiss the seriousness of mental abuse, rationalizing it as a petty argument between husband and wife, and saying it's not serious unless he hits her. In reality, mental abuse does severe psychological harm to many Muslim women.[40]

Memon continues to say that, though domestic abuse is totally unacceptable in Islam, "For cultural reasons, some Muslim men accept the idea that it's normal for a man to hit his wife and that she is no more than a piece of his property."[41] Imams are of little help either, says Memon. They advise abused women to pray for the abuse to end and to be patient. Some even accuse the woman of being responsible for bringing on the abuse and make them feel guilty and send them back home to their abuser. Some imams misinterpret Islam's emphasis on family privacy and tell women to keep family matters to themselves. "The imams' reactions stem from ignorance, cowardice, or friendship or blood relationship with the abusive husbands. Relatively few imams have had the wisdom and courage to tackle the problem head-on." As a result of this, many abused women don't bother turning to imams for help.[42]

Women like Adam and Ibrahim are there to help another Muslim woman face the problem without feeling ashamed. Adam says, "It helps that I'm Muslim so I can say to her, 'I'm Muslim too.'"[43] It is common sense that counseling to deal with these issues would be better performed by fellow Muslims because they would be aware of Islamic culture, attitudes, and family life.

Both organizations have many success stories. *Apna Ghar* and *Niswa* have fought hard to rebuild the lives of women and children who are abused physically and emotionally, a difficult task considering both shelters' aim is to keep families together peacefully. Both Ibrahim and Adam emphasize that what their shelter needs most, though, is money to pay for legal services, improvements to the overutilized shelters, and employment of additional staff to handle an increasing workload.[44] Memon says that currently, the American Muslim community only covers about a quarter of community needs in this area.[45] Other Muslim social service organizations are emerging to fill nationwide voids in health care and other areas.[46] It's people like Ibrahim and Adam, though they are immigrant Muslim women, who are truly living the American spirit of civic duty.

Many opportunities for American Muslim women to unify as a group are occurring today. With more young Muslim women attending college, they will interact with a variety of Muslim women (and men) and perhaps learn to function as a group of

American Muslim women and not as representatives of their culture only.

In addition, as the shortage of men within a particular ethnic group continues, a fact true for both Palestinians and African-Americans, young women with their mothers' blessings will sacrifice a shared heritage with their spouse for shared religion with their spouse, as it should be in America.[47] Ethnic groups will be less clannish as more interethnic marriages take place, leading to interethnic unity and support among Muslim women.

Already, American Muslim women born to immigrant families call themselves feminists, and their families do not reject, in fact accept, them for their views.[48] Perhaps someday, mothers may even see higher education as more than bait for a suitable husband but as a means of empowerment and improvement for their daughters.

A small minority of American Muslims say Americanization and the mixing of the sexes among American Muslims will come to an end, that the progress Muslim women have made will cease as American Muslims become even more conservative. I believe that view is incorrect.

The Islamic principles of ethnic and gender equality are being tested in America, and the combination of American activism and women's liberation according to the Qur'an will continue to bring American Muslim women together. From the emotionally and intellectually charged debate over *hijab* (see Close-Up) to a suburban Muslim family contemplating a proposal of arranged marriage, the choices of Muslim women will serve as a barometer of Islam's future in America, and the signs are, in many respects, highly promising.

CLOSE-UP
Free to Be a Muslim Feminist

A few facts make me believe that the Prophet Muhammad was one of the world's first feminists and that Islam is a feminist's religion. He banned female infanticide, deeming it a sin in Islam. It was a bold move for his time, as pre-Islamic patriarchal culture prompted parents to bury their female offspring, seen as useless in comparison to a son who could provide for the family. Muhammad even said that any man who raises, provides for, and educates two daughters has a spot reserved for him in Heaven. In addition, Muhammad's wife, Khadijah, played an important role in Islam, as discussed in chapter six. Furthermore, what we have learned about Muhammad, the major proponent of Islam, is from the women in his life, his wives and daughters—who later became leaders of the faith and important sources of information on his life. Can you see how easy it is for a Muslim woman to be a feminist now? Islam, from its inception, has always been about elevating the status of women, even before such a notion was a Western ideal.

CLOSE-UP
The Long Road for Female Converts to Islam

Female converts face the additional problem of rejection by their birth family. Families often blame the Muslim husband. Carol Anway says that many families declare their daughters to be dead and refuse to see them. If families do maintain relations with their converted daughters, the relationships are often strained by the daughters' worries over eating *halal* (Islamically proscribed food and food preparation). A major complaint for converts in Anway's survey is that they are uncomfortable leaving their children with their parents, though they need the assistance, because of the fear of their children consuming non-*halal* food. Acceptance by converts' families took anywhere from three to thirteen years among Anway's respondents. Many converts' stories eventually have happy endings: "After my thirteen years of marriage [and conversion], she [convert's mother] told me that I looked beautiful in my head scarf, just like the statues of the Virgin Mary."[1] But it's not an easy road for female converts. Those who convert without being married have trouble finding a husband. Many Muslim men wish to marry in their own culture, leaving white female American converts alone.

CLOSE-UP
Hijab in America: Why Won't Westerners Understand?

I was having my hair "wrapped" in Piccadilly Circus in London, which means a set of colored strings was being woven into small braids in my hair. Sitting on a plastic milk cart a few inches off the ground, I had been blabbing away to Kevin, the man wrapping my hair. He seemed to know every non-tourist who walked by, culminating with a drunk Londoner who smelled as if he needed to shower and change his clothes. He commenced harassing tourists with the hairbrush he was carrying (but apparently hadn't thought of using himself) and trying to scare me.

A woman wearing *hijab* noticed the wrapping and stopped to watch. "How neat," she said, looking at me and Kevin as she walked away. "Damn Muslims!" Kevin said. "What?" I asked, pulling my hair away from his grip and looking up at him. "Those Muslims, covering their hair!" he said exasperatedly. "It's just not right!"

I have the dubious fortune of being able to listen to people insult my culture or my religion in front of me, as they do not know that I am those things they have just ranted about. I am soon employed in dispelling stereotypes. "I'm Muslim!" I said. "You are?" asked Kevin, astounded. "No, you're not!" He answered for me. How could I, this person he thought was normal and whom he liked, be a *Muslim?* How could I be one of those backward people?

"Yes, I am!" I declared with zest. "Well, you're not *hardcore,* like that girl was," Kevin said matter-of-factly, as if covering my hair would suddenly make me a hardcore Muslim. I don't know if Kevin and others expect me to appreciate that they think I'm normal while other Muslim women, not much different from me except that they wear *hijab,* are crazy and un-Western. I tried to explain to Kevin that certainly in the Western world *hijab* is a choice and not representative of terrorism and Islamic fundamentalism, as he and others no doubt see it. But I don't think I was able to convey these feelings to him.

Why couldn't I explain myself to Kevin, though? Westerners like him tolerate everything in their society: drug-users, drunks, smelly friends who scare away customers. They are open to those practicing alternative lifestyles. We criticize the International Olympic Committee for having rules against marijuana that discriminate against snowboarders. Yet why are we so averse to *hijab* when we celebrate nearly everything else? First, I think we subscribe to the stereotype that Muslim women are oppressed as a population. To some extent, it is true that Muslim women living in Islamic countries have the short end of the stick. Literacy is appallingly low, birth control is hard to come by, and patriarchy often reigns in Islamic countries. However, none of these facts has any direct connection to Islam or the Qur'an. (Female genital mutilation, for instance, a remnant of African tribal custom is practiced in many African, Islamic countries, though the Qur'an would clearly forbid such activity.) In fact, Islam extended rights to women at a time when such progress for women was unheard of: right to property, inheritance, education, divorce, child custody among other things. Patriarchal culture that existed in these countries before Islam has become ingrained with the interpretation of some Qur'anic passages. Add that to the plight of a country that is already poor and rural, as many Muslim countries are, and, of course, Islam *appears to be* the great oppressor of women when actually many non-religious factors contribute to women's suffering in those countries.

The problem is, when Kevin sees a woman wearing *hijab*, like many of us living in the West, he sees a woman who is inherently foreign, uneducated, and oppressed, as if the head cover were an instant indicator of those traits. Media emphasis on stereotypes of the oppressed Muslim woman has caused this stilted view. At best, we Westerners associate an exotic mystique with *hijab,* acknowledging women who wear *hijab* as alien and different.

Americans and Westerners see *hijab* as repressive and symbolic proof of the oppression of Muslim women. Nothing could be further from the truth with many American Muslim women. I admit that some are compelled by community peer pressure to wear *hijab,* and then the focus on wearing *hijab* as an act of faith and devotion to God is lost. But for all those blindly wearing *hijab,* an equal or higher number of women who are intelligent and powerful *choose* to wear *hijab.* To some, this is a way of fulfilling a request from God, as Protestant women go through Confirmation or Catholics accept Communion.

What makes Western inability to understand *hijab* so funny to me is that the practice originated in Europe and is a part of Western culture. Though seen as an Islamic act, *hijab* has its roots in a time long before the existence of Islam. Ancient Greek women draped their heads to indicate their wealthy status. In medieval Europe, women are said to have covered their heads to show they were of the upper class. Today, Queen Elizabeth is rarely seen without a scarf tied around her head, and, were the Queen Muslim, she would be wearing *hijab* too! By no means is *hijab* a reflection of tendencies toward terrorism or violence. If we believed so, what would that make the Virgin Mary, who is always portrayed as wearing a scarf, look like?

The main point of *hijab* is to preserve modesty as requested of both men and women in the Qur'an. But I don't wear *hijab* myself because I don't think God is asking me to. In the Prophet Muhammad's time, only his wives wore *hijab*, and, after his death, upper-class women wore *hijab*, attempting to emulate the status of the Prophet's wives.[1] I know that to be accepted within conservative Muslim circles you must wear *hijab.* But like Westerners, some Muslims focus entirely too much on what's on a woman's head rather than what is inside it.

That is precisely one of the cons of wearing *hijab*—you're treated like a second-class citizen. Everyone assumes covered women can be cheated out of change, ignored, or sneered at. It's amazing to me that we tolerate a variety of morally lax activities in society such as bars and pubs on every corner, swearing in public, forcing condoms on pre-teens, Hooters in suburbia, *Hustler* sold on the same rack as *TV Guide,* and men unabashedly leafing through the nonsealed pornographic magazines at public newsstands, yet we are appalled at the sight of someone who is religious. I'm not attacking people for drinking or swearing or enjoying a little pornography. I'm not a right-wing, family values freak. I'm just saying that Americans and Westerners only accept what they understand, particularly giving in to one's desires and emotions, and believe in secularism, publicly accepting habits we all agree are fun and enjoyable but nodding our heads and tsk-tsking in disapproval at individual expression we don't understand or recognize as a matter of choice.

── 7 ◆ Growing Up in America: Creating New World Islam ──

As with all communities, each subgroup within Islam has its own culturally enhanced idea of what aspects of Islam are most important. Of course, we all agree on the basic tenets of Islam, such as the Five Pillars and the Five Articles of Faith; we agree that there is one God and that Muhammad is his messenger.

However, despite those unifying points, different Muslim ethnic groups emphasize some things more than others. For example, Saudi Arabians emphasize women's modesty much more than other cultures do, as women in Saudi Arabia wear head-to-toe covers, are often segregated from men at gatherings, and are not allowed to drive. I, as an American, read the Qur'an from a different perspective and do not think that women need to be so separated from mainstream society.

It's all a matter of how one looks at things based on one's cultural background. Every world culture focuses on different sets of values. We see this in the United States. A friend of mine who lives in the South has two roommates who are black, something that causes controversy among his neighbors because my friend is white. Because of their racial mix these three roommates are seen as strange by their fellow townsfolk. When I was explaining this situation to my mom and my brother, they both, as usual, tried to finish my thought before I could. "This friend of mine— he's white—and has two black roommates. They live in the South, and my friend says they 'raise eyebrows around town.'"

"Oh," my mom blurted out, "so they're gay."

"Yeah, they're gay, right?" my brother added.

"Noooo," I announced. "The people in the South are upset that a white person is living with a black person."

"Ohhhhh," said Ali and mom in unison, drawing the word out into a second syllable.

Why did both my mom and my brother think that the towns-folk would assume that two black men and one white man living together would be gay? I thought racism was a more obvious reason. But I realized that in Colorado, where my brother grew up and my mom has lived for over twenty years, racism is probably not as much on our minds as homophobia. Many family-values, right-wing organizations are headquartered in Colorado, and they are anti-gay-rights.

Varying emphases by region (like Colorado versus the South) and cultural background cause a variety of supplemental beliefs. This is what has happened with Islam. While all Muslims agree on the basic tenets, we have different values we empha-size, and different customs and traditions. A wedding in Pakistan is very different from an Indonesian wedding, which are both different from an Iranian wedding, though all three are Muslim countries.

Here in America, we have Muslims from countries all over the world with their own interpretations. We also have kids like me who grew up here with significantly less ethnic cultural influence. For example, Muslim mothers and daughters, both in immigrant families and in families who have converted, struggle over how independent a daughter should be. The mothers came from or converted to a setting that was quite conservative, yet the daughters grew up in more liberal times, and want more independence as a result. That's what Islam in America is all about: Muslims from all over the world coming together and thereby losing emphasis on their native cultures and working together to find an understanding of Islam that we all agree on. Young Muslims are an integral part of this new world Islam. It is my generation, the children of immigrants and converts, some converts themselves, who must figure out what it means to be Muslim in America.

We must distinguish between what is culture and what is religion. In order to be both American and Muslim, we are going to have to let go of certain aspects of our ethnic cultures, of Islam, and of our American culture. If we don't make some hard choices we'll end up being confused and in denial. I can't ignore the fact that I'm Pakistani, or that I'm Muslim, or that I am an American. Yet it is a great challenge to strike a balance among those value systems. We will strike that balance by choosing what is important to us from among our various value systems.

American Muslims don't have the cultural support system most Muslims all over the world have. Each Islamic country has its own set of Qur'anic interpretations, even a group of academics that set those interpretations, called the *ulema*. Here in the United States, Muslims are mostly flying blind, although we do have a national Fiqh Council, created by and consisting of some American Muslim leaders. The council is available to answer questions about practicing Islam in America and is trying to position itself as an American *ulema*. So far, the council has not played a significant role. We do have the Qur'an and some other Islamic writings, which we can use as compasses, indicators of how we can conduct ourselves. However, we need to create our own support systems to go with our new approaches to the Qur'an. I think that full-time Islamic schools, along with mosques, help us create such a support system.

I have been part of an E-mail distribution list for the past few years run by the Muslim Public Affairs Council (MPAC), meaning we send E-mails to a particular address, and everyone on the list receives the E-mail. It's like an electronic discussion. Ideally, the group members meet a few times a year in person, set goals, and then discuss their progress over E-mail. As with most distribution lists, we often move into debates that divide the group and are slightly off-topic.

In coming years, the American Muslim community will be strengthened by this ability to communicate so directly and so often. CyberIslam can be a great support system for American Muslims, with Frequently Asked Questions posted on websites like www.theprophetonline.com or E-mail to hadith@sunna.com. A global, electronic *ulema* will probably emerge. Already, we have excellent Islamic websites like www.islam.org, which provides Qur'anic search engines as well as several other Islamic tools. Run by a group of Muslim interpreneurs, www.islam.org conducted the first live broadcast of the pilgrimage to Mecca ever. Over three million people visit the website, including me, for its online Qur'an and recitations. Besides www.islam.org and other Islamic websites, Muslims can even send online religious greetings with www.mubarakgreetings.com and from the popular free E-card website www.bluemountain.com. Eventually, Islamic full-time schooling may be conducted over the Internet, easing the pressure Islamic schools face over scarce resources like facilities and teaching staff.[1] However, we will probably run into problems of how the message of Islam is spread online. Currently, while many websites on Islam have accurate information, others do not. As with all websites, you have to read each site carefully before you take the information there as all true.

On the MPAC distribution list, a debate began with a message from a man who seemed to suggest that American Muslims needed to come up with solutions to the problem of what young Muslims should do who are not being allowed to date because of Islamic traditions, yet are not marrying at a young age. Was there any room for dating in American Islam, he was asking. I believe he was alluding to the fact that young people want companionship, intimate companionship, but aren't really sure they can have that without being condemned by fellow Muslims. It's a valid question because, if we aren't totally arranging marriages of young Muslims, how are they supposed to meet each other? I respected this man's bravery in speaking out in this forum. We all have this issue on our minds, but who wants to bring it up on an E-mail distribution list?

Almost immediately, a few members of the group responded resolutely along the lines of: "There is no premarital sex in Islam, and we shouldn't waste our time talking about this." One woman explained why sex outside of marriage is forbidden in Islam, for very good reasons. It is meant to bring stability to the community. She quoted Dr. Hassan Hathout of the Islamic Center of Southern California as saying that sex outside of marriage is forbidden in Islam because Islam stands for justice between women and men. Sex outside of marriage is an injustice against women, as any negative consequences of such actions are almost totally shouldered by them, specifically pregnancy. In addition, a few offered that the Prophet's solution to carnal desires was to fast, to learn patience and self-control, and to marry, even at a young age. That was about all they said.

Technically, there is no *explicit* prohibition against premarital sex in the Qur'an, but there are several implicit indicators against it: encouragement of marriage at a young age, modesty in appearance, and so on. Masturbation is also discouraged. One is instructed to fast to control urges. Basically, if you want to have sex and be a good Muslim, you should get married.

This discussion was taking place at the time of the public disclosure of President Clinton's affair with former White House intern Monica Lewinsky. Most on the distribution list seemed to be saying regarding infidelity and sexual misconduct, that we shouldn't talk about sex when there were more important things going in the country and world.

But, I was upset that this issue wasn't taken more seriously. What I mean is that we American Muslims should be talking about how we can solve this issue, not about fasting and marrying at the age of sixteen. So I had what my brother calls a "spaz" and let my feelings known over the Internet.

I wrote in a huff that I thought this topic was really important for a bunch of reasons that I hadn't coherently organized as yet. First of all, it would have been silly for me to get married as soon as I realized I was attracted to men. In the Prophet's time, 1,400 years ago in Arabia, people married around the age of fifteen anyway because they only expected to live to their mid-30s. Second, I want to marry a Muslim and have Muslim kids, yet most of the Muslim boys I met socially and actually had a chance to get to know were "players." I don't think their primary interest was marriage. Third, I wasn't meeting nice Muslim boys who weren't interested in premarital sex because at every event I went to at a mosque, where there might be such boys, we were segregated by gender! So what is a young Muslim girl to do?

Especially when, fourth, I had noticed that many young Muslim women I knew who had dated and had premarital sex with Muslims and non-Muslims were now marrying nice Muslim men. They became acquainted with these boys by dating them, and now they're marrying them. Good girls like me were, as Tom Petty once sang, "sitting home with broken hearts" and had little prospect of a marriage we'd be pleased with. Furthermore, some of the players, who were the children of immigrant Muslims usually, would eventually ask their mothers to find them nice girls from their home country, not girls like me who were supposedly already corrupted by American life.

I had a few more thoughts that I didn't add, but my frustration was evident. I'm not yet ready to get married, but why shouldn't I develop relationships, maybe not more than friendship or dating without sex (if that's possible), that could develop into marriage? Why do I have to live like a nun with no companionship until I consent to an arranged marriage? Especially when many Muslim boys are dating and having sex with non-Muslim women because the community doesn't come down as hard on them. Many Muslims have a double standard in disciplining girls versus disciplining boys on such matters. Why should I marry young to fulfill desires but risk my education and career for a family? Furthermore, why is arranged marriage a viable alternative? I'm supposed to marry any boy who charms my parents enough?

Later, I came across a *Minaret* magazine survey of 90 Muslim students in California colleges on premarital sex. My suspicions that barring Muslim youth from each other causes Muslim youth to socialize with non-Muslim youth were somewhat confirmed. Sixty percent had engaged in some sort of physical intimacy without involving sex with non-Muslims; only 6.6 percent had with other Muslims; 28.8 percent had had premarital sex with non-Muslims; 4.4 percent with Muslims. Clearly the goal is not for Muslims to have sex or intimacy only with each other, but to create an environment where Muslims are not turning away from their religion.

Things are different in America. Men and women, boys and girls, meet all the time, in the mall, at work, in school. We can't isolate ourselves from that. Even if we cover a woman from head to toe and tell her to stay in the house all day, at some point, she'll have to call the plumber because the toilet's overflowing, and the plumber could easily be a man. American culture is challenging us as Muslims: how contemporary can we be? How will we solve this problem? The first step, for many, is admitting we have a problem. It's more than condemning pre-marital sex. As an American and a woman who wants some semblance of a career, I don't really believe in marriage at a young age. As a Muslim, I don't want to become morally lax.

I don't want to have my parents arranging a marriage for me in my thirties. At the same time, many Muslims insist that the Qur'an does not allow for Muslim men and women who are not related to each other to meet. As a young woman who has grown up in America, I'm not willingly going to consent to an "old world" arranged marriage like my mother had. At the same time, I know, as a Muslim and Pakistani, that I'm certainly not free to date, meet (and probably have sex with) men. So how do I marry if I don't intend on having an arranged marriage, yet I'm not ready to turn my back on cultural and religious standards against dating?

Early marriage is not the solution. One man wrote, in our E-mail discussion, that, "Most (but not all) of the sexual-urge-hastened marriages that I've seen have broken up miserably in 1 to 3 years, or are mired in despair and miscommunication." Obviously that's not what we want. He said he was concerned for older Muslim women who were not meeting nice Muslim men because the communities are often segregated. One female friend of his "questions whether or not she has to 'be *haram* [unlawful] now in order to be *halal* [lawful] for the rest of my life.'" He ends by saying, "I think we've reached a point where the Muslim youth of America have to establish communities that are separate from *masjids* [mosques; his point is that mosques will not allow men and women to meet because of Islamic guidelines] in order to foster effective and indigenous social services, promote intellectually free and challenging discourse, and create healthy and Islamic interaction between the sexes."

Some Muslims say that you can meet a member of the opposite sex within Islamic guidelines. You must only be sincere in your interest in marrying this person. You can't just shoot the breeze and hang out with them for the hell of it. As a result, first meetings are loaded with expectation. The man who began the discussion pointed out that we need to move away from this idea of relationships between genders as only leading to marriage and allow men and women to meet accepting, in his words, "the possibility that things would not work out." One woman wrote of girls to whom she teaches sex education, who say that young Muslim men are justifying as Islamic all sorts of sexual escapades, especially engaging in premarital intimacy without intercourse, whereas these same men look down on women who engage in similar activities as un-Islamic. She calls this "an abuse of our religion . . . a form of self-deception" concluding that the Prophet was open to all topics, including sexuality, and that we should try to be "creative and courageous" in these "challenging times."

In Britain, Pakistani women who refuse to marry boys their families pick for them are so severely punished, sometimes burnt with acid or beaten, and threatened that they run away from home. Families hire bounty hunters to find them and send them immediately to Pakistan. Officials find these cases "alarmingly common."[2] We certainly don't want what's happening in Britain to happen here. We need to strike a balance between the traditions of Islam and the freedoms of Western culture. They should not be so dissimilar as to result in life and death situations, and we, as American Muslims, should be strong enough to overcome the difficulties and challenges.

Currently American Muslims regard sex the way American Catholics regard abortion: though everyone else in America does it, we can't because it's against our belief system, although many do it on the sly anyway. While Catholics can quixotically try to pressure the Pope to ease up on the Church's antiabortion stance, Muslims do not have a central authority to appeal to. Muslims, at this point, have only themselves and each other to answer to, which makes what I call "Muslim guilt" all the worse. We want our kids to meet each other and marry, but we're scared they'll descend into self-gratifying, destructive behavior!

Really, the issue manifests itself between Muslim parents and children today in arguments over going to the school dance. Right now, I'd say many Muslim families' attitudes are "don't ask; don't tell."

Nevertheless, American Muslims are curious as to what is and what is not allowed under Islam. My brother, Ali, has an hilarious story about trying to buy a book on Islam's view of sex. At the very back of a catalog of Islamic books, he found under "Miscellaneous" two items regarding Islam and sex. One was a large book on the topic called something like *The Islamic View of Sex.* The second item was a small pamphlet with a similar title. So Ali called the Islamic book company to order the large book. "Whenever you name the title of the book you want, the man from the book company says something like '*Mashallah,* that is a wonderful book!'" Ali said, mimicking an immigrant accent for the man who was taking his call. "But when I asked for the book on sex, he got really quiet. Then he said [imagine Ali's accent again], 'I am sorry brother, but we are out of that book right now.'" We would all laugh at Ali's imitation of this man shamefully saying that the one book they had on sex was, of all things, sold out! How embarrassing! Ali adds at the end of this story, "So I'm not the only Muslim who is wondering about sex!"

As sexual liberation arrived in America, so did Muslims. Muslim immigrants from many countries poured into America during the late sixties and early seventies. The children of these immigrants, first generation American Muslims, are dealing with the issue of sex head-on. At first, Muslims living in America lucked out a bit, depending on your definition of "luck." Since they were already living in America, in a modern setting, they didn't feel the need to adopt American ideas of dating and sex to modernize themselves. At the same time, Muslim parents emphasized family activities and kept their sons and especially their daughters at home on prom night.

In a strange twist of fate, parents like mine created a little Pakistan (or whatever country Muslim immigrants came from) for their kids—conservative and strict, while Pakistan (or the immigrant parents' country) itself was undergoing a sexual revolution to some extent. Parents like mine missed out on the sexual revolution in their own country and made an effort not to be a part of it in America. The only man my mother ever kissed was my father. She married when she was eighteen. The parents of today's Black Muslims had similarly conservative upbringings in Elijah Muhammad's NOI. Imagine asking them for advice on birth control!

If dating means having a sexual relationship, clearly Muslims are against dating. As conservative parents preserved for us a version of the culture they grew up in—meaning no dating, no meeting between genders outside of family—the cultures of our parents and American culture moved on without us. Now what do we do?

I see four possibilities. Each of these potential outcomes is important because each one indicates *how* Americans have assimilated into American culture and if American Muslims have succeeded in assimilating appropriately. The first possibility is that nothing will change; "don't ask; don't tell" will reign. This also means that many American Muslims may not be marrying other Muslims. Considering the next two possibilities, this one has some appeal.

The second possibility is that American Muslims will change their attitudes toward dating and come closer to most Americans' understanding of dating. American Muslims will allow their children to have premarital sex, and probably live with other people. This is not really a desirable outcome because American Muslims will lose many other characteristics that are important to community identity like marrying Muslims or converted Muslims. If American Muslims are less firm in their stance against premarital sex, about what else will they weaken? How much of their beliefs will they follow? Will they all be Eid Muslims, meaning Muslims who only attend mosque on major holidays? Will more marry outside of Islam? A tangent to this possibility is that American Muslims will focus less on what Islam has to say about sex—it's not a whole lot anyway—and focus more on other aspects of Islam that are central to the religion like the Five Pillars. This tangent makes this possibility a little more desirable.

If American Muslims openly condone premarital sex among their children, then they will have to deal with Muslim guilt. This will be hard; some Muslim men, particularly male members of NOI, are consumed with the idea of preserving their daughters' and sisters' virginity. They will have to convince themselves that abstinence and preservation of a women's virginity are not the most important tenets of Islam and that Allah won't call us on this on the big day.

The third possibility is that American Muslims will increasingly encourage their children to marry young and within the faith, as soon as their hormones and desires kick in, even as young as eighteen. Aversion to early marriage in America, is primarily due to the belief that it will result in divorce and/or weaken one's career aspirations and achievements. American Muslims have the same aversion.

In the process however, Muslims may realize or rediscover that, in Islam, divorce is not forbidden. From a Qur'anic point of view, no stigma is attached to divorce. It is only Muslim people who, living in their various cultures, have come to see divorce as a bad thing. That is not to say that Muslims should not aim for a marriage to last; certainly they should and do. But Islam does not want Muslims to remain unhappy in unhappy marriages— divorce is allowed and encouraged in that situation. As my mother put it, Catholicism and other religions encourage marriage and discourage divorce; Islam encourages marriage *and* divorce when necessary. So Muslims could potentially marry young, for the companionship and sex, and, if things don't work out, they could divorce. Later on, divorcees could re-marry others. They would have done all this within the guidelines of Islam.

American Muslims must choose how they want their future to be. If they want to grow as Americans and Muslims though, I do not think they can let the present situation, "don't ask; don't tell," continue for much longer. I always ask myself, what will I do with my own kids—will I let them go on dates? Is it more important to me that they don't date, or that they do not turn away from Islam? Or by dating would they automatically not be Muslims?

The fourth possibility and maybe the most attractive is that the growth of the American Muslim community will run parallel to the model of other religious groups. Mormons and other American religious groups have opened their own universities and created other environments, where young members of the faith meet, date, and marry. The important thing is that they meet each other (and realize the community expectations against premarital sex). This outcome is also desirable for Muslims—creating their own prestigious university with the goal of educating Muslims and preserving their morals. But it is also at least five to ten years away. Muslims lack the infrastructure and resources at this time to create a BYU of their own.

So where do American Muslims draw the line? When is enough *enough?* When are so many traditions and values thrown by the wayside that we are no longer practicing Islam? Or that we have assimilated like some American Jews, arguably, beyond recognition? When does the de facto Reform Islam we American Muslims are practicing—by only attending mosque on Eid, by not covering our heads, by dating, by not praying five times a day, by not eating *halal* (Islamically proscribed) food—become seriously un-Islamic behavior? Already, we are seeing mixed-faith marriages. What happens when a boy with a Muslim mother and Christian father starts dating a girl whose mom was converted as a Reform Jew? What if the couple decides they want to be Buddhist? What will their wedding ceremony be like?

It's obviously confusing, and, while I look forward to having children, I am concerned about how and whether I can raise them as American Muslims. I am also wondering if I'll ever meet a Muslim boy I'd like to marry, as every event I attend where there are marriageable Muslim boys, the group is segregated by gender. Muslim men marry non-Muslim women all the time. What's a girl to do when she's not allowed to date, yet she can't meet boys of her own faith? I feel strongly that Muslim boys and girls should be encouraged to meet, even date, if we, as a Muslim community, want to have Muslim grandkids. This is the beauty of America, though: we are all here, together, striking a balance in our lives between competing desires. That is how American Muslim youth will have to grow up: finding and striking a balance they can live with.

CLOSE-UP
Whither Reform Islam? What American Muslims Can Learn from American Jews

A plausible model of adjustment to American life is an assimilation similar to the kind American Jews have experienced. Some feel that the creation of Reform Judaism was the greatest catalyst to Jews' assimilation, but a similar outcome is not possible for American Muslims. When Rabbi Isaac Mayer Wise proposed the idea of Reform Judaism, it made, and still makes, much sense. Wise proposed that Jews adopt a "reformed" version of Judaism that would make life in America easier for Jews. Jews could still practice Judaism without having such practice interfere in their daily lives as Americans. Under Reform Judaism, Jewish men do not have to wear yarmulkes at all times. Jews do not have to observe kosher dietary laws, can work on Saturdays, and so on. Today, Reform Judaism emphasizes the importance of the individual in interpreting Judaism.

While the American Jewish population is recognized by all for its achievements, its influence and prominence, financial and personal success, many Jews are worried that Jews have assimilated too well, so much so that their identity as Jews is no longer separate from American society itself. For example, Craig Horowitz writes in a *New York* magazine cover story called "The Disappearance of American Jews" that ten or fifteen years ago, a show like "Seinfeld" would have been too whiny, too neurotic, in short, too Jewish even to be considered as a sitcom. Now, the Jewish humor of the television show *Seinfeld* is enjoyed by mostly non-Jewish Americans.[1] The result of this assimilation has been a decline in the number of American Jews, due in part to intermarriage with Gentiles. The result has been a loss in understanding what it means to be a Jew, a "spiritual holocaust," as Rabbi Ephraim Buchweld calls it in Horowitz's article.[2] Clearly American Muslims do not want to lose their community identity and should try to learn from the American Jewish experience.

Whether Reform is an appropriate way to practice Judaism is not a matter for me to decide, but I recognize the value of Reform

Judaism. It did make it easier for Jews to function in American society. It broke down the barriers and taboos Orthodox Judaism held in regard to American lifestyle. I know my life would certainly be easier if I didn't have to worry about informing waiters at restaurants that I cannot eat ham, bacon, pork, or food prepared with lard. If a "Reform Islam" existed, I wouldn't have to worry about this issue and a few other aspects of Muslim life.

However, "Reform Islam" cannot exist for the simple reason that Muslims, as a group, cannot set up Islamic doctrine. Islam itself, and American Islam, have no real structure for such widespread reinterpretation. Most Islamic countries, as I have said, have a group of religious scholars, called the *ulema,* who interpret Islam for their country. American Muslims don't have an *ulema.* As a result, Muslims don't have a governing authority who can "decree" a "Reform Islam." In truth, Islam is really supposed to be practiced and interpreted by each individual and not handed down by a Pope-like figure. It says so in the Qur'an.

In a sense, Islam is already "reformed" because of the Islamic emphasis on individual interpretation. Sunni Islam, the sect of Islam that about 90 percent of the world's Muslims follow, is a fairly moderate, practically "reform" version itself, even including the dietary restrictions, as compared to the less moderate Shi'ite sect. It really gets down to the issue of dating and marriage. The balance that American Muslims have struck between American culture and Islam is, in essence, a de facto Reform Islam. But Islam does not have *that many rules* that come into major conflict with American life. Many Qur'anic requirements fit in well with American life if the Muslim makes an effort to fit them in. Muslims are expected to have jobs and provide for their families. Muslims believe that you should respect the government you live under because that government provides for you. Additionally, the Qur'an lists provisions in the event that some duties cannot be done. For example, if you are traveling for business or school during the month of Ramadan, you can make up that day's fast on another day. So a "Reform Islam" isn't essential to the American Muslim's existence.

CLOSE-UP
Full-Time Islamic Schools: Making Growing Up Muslim in America Easier

Full-time Islamic schools, which total about 200 nationwide, are preferred by about a quarter of immigrant American Muslims, according to Yvonne Haddad and Adair Lummis, and are seen as instrumental in increasing the self-confidence of young Muslims.[1] At least forty of these schools are through the twelfth grade according to the Council of Islamic Schools in North America. Islamic education is the same as any other school's curriculum except that it emphasizes principles based on the Qur'an and the *sunna* [habits] of the Prophet, including learning Arabic, and Islamic practice and prayer. Islamic schools are also, to Muslim parents, a haven from the negative aspects of American culture, such as drinking, premarital sex, gangs, and so on. At the same time, Muslim children can benefit from being in America, in the free and open American classroom setting.

I have spent some time researching the newest branch of the New Horizon School system in Los Angeles. The system consists of three Islamic schools, founded by the Islamic Center of Southern California. The first school in the network was established in Pasadena, the second in Los Angeles, located inside the Islamic Center. The third and newest New Horizon school is in Orange County. The New Horizon Schools are "committed to providing children with . . . quality academic education based on high moral values in an Islamic environment." Like other full-time Islamic schools, they focus on helping students strike a balance between Islam and American culture and modernity: "Our aim is to prepare our students to effectively deal with the challenges of a modern society."[2] As a result of this focus, the New Horizon Schools, and probably many other Islamic schools, fulfills Turkish sociologist Zia Gökalp's educational ideal: to teach the "culture and value commitments . . . unique to every society" and general education as well.[3]

Besides teaching Arabic, Qur'anic studies, prayer, and other aspects of practicing Islam, Islamic schools are also different from many other American schools in that the teacher-student ratio is small, creating a familial environment. In addition, the atmosphere is more disciplined and supportive because of the small class size. At first, Islamic schools had some difficulty in gaining enrollment because they often did not advertise. But as word spread and the schools began advertising, enrollment numbers and demand usually increased, resulting in long waiting lists. As a result, many Islamic schools want to upgrade campuses to meet the now huge demand.

Why are full-time Islamic schools so popular? Mainly because they help Muslim parents raise their children as American Muslims. Parents of kids at the New Horizon Schools do not have the extra burden of explaining why the Easter Bunny doesn't come to their home. Their children's' teachers explain such things already at school in a manner that kids can understand.

Islamic schools also enhance a young Muslim's ability to practice and believe in Islam. They include Arabic in their curriculum and may bring about a reverse in the decline of Arabic literacy, a trend noticeable among Palestinian and other immigrants.[4] Fazlur Rahman, in his book *Islam and Modernity,* feels that teaching Arabic highlights "the original sources of Islam, the Qur'an and the Hadith."[5] His opinion is particularly important in the United States where cultural interpretations of Islam can and should be overshadowed by an emphasis on Arabic and the Qur'an. An additional benefit for students is that participating in Ramadan, the Islamic month of fasting, is probably easier on them, thereby avoiding "the peer pressure" some parents feel their children face in public schools during Ramadan.[6]

This is not to say that Muslim parents can't raise their kids without sending them to an Islamic school. Obviously they can. My parents did. However, an Islamic school makes the burden of raising Muslims in a country filled with Christian images, symbols, role models, television characters, and so on, a little easier. Islamic schools are similar to Catholic schools or other parochial schools in emphasizing the importance of one's own religion. An Islamic school has the same goals as does a Catholic school—to create an environment that is still very American but is sheltered from influences that work against Islam and Catholicism or that make kids feel "weird" and different being a Muslim or Catholic.

Imam Gasser Hathout of the Orange County Islamic Center conducts the *Juma* (Friday) prayers at the New Horizon School delivering a *khutba* or sermon, which I observed. Imam Hathout and the ethnically diverse student body of the New Horizon School followed a format typical of Islamic practice with the exception that students retold Imam Hathout's sermon after the group prayed.[7] After the students prayed, with another young student serving as *muezzin,* or the person who performs the call to prayer, the young Muslims alternated in retelling Imam Hathout's *khutba.* They eagerly raised their hands, one after the other, wanting to express what they had learned.[8] The students handled the theologically important aspects of the *adhan,* or call to prayer, and the prayer itself, by themselves, and reveled in learning about and telling a theologically significant story. In this American Islamic school, the students were able to explore their religious duties and beliefs freely, accepting their mistakes in retelling the sermon and practicing their religion without shame or feeling alienated from the rest of the class. The event is moving for those American Muslims who feel Islam is losing the battle against American culture. The New Horizon School's *Juma* prayer is a first step in helping young Muslims create and accept a positive American Muslim identity.

The most important result of attending an Islamic school probably cannot be measured in a standardized test but is seen throughout one's life; the Muslims who have attended Islamic schools may prove to be more confident and well-adjusted. Sonsyrea Tate writes in her book *Little X: Growing Up in the Nation of Islam* that NOI schools made the young NOI members feel good about themselves: "Now that Elijah Muhammad had convinced them that they weren't hoodlums but children of God, they were absolutely fearless." After attending a predominantly African-American public high school for a few years after her NOI school closed, Tate noticed that she was more advanced than her peers, having accelerated two years.[9] The students currently attending the Orange County New Horizon school seem to be particularly advanced intellectually for their age. Of the students interviewed who had previously attended American public schools, most say they have more friends and feel they fit in better at the New Horizon school than they did at their previous school.[10] The students I interviewed also seemed quite talkative and confident for their age.[11]

Islamic schooling brings the practice of Islam into the world outside of one's home. Living in Colorado, I could now send my children (when I have them) to Denver's Crescent View Academy—an Islamic school that has been homegrown in the Rocky Mountains. The Islamic base adult Muslims will turn to as they enter society is strengthened, encouraging lifelong Islamic practice. For this reason, many American Muslims feel they should open Islamic high schools, particularly because one's identity is most challenged during the difficult teenage years. Finally, Islamic schools provide a setting where young Muslim boys and girls can meet each other without the conservative members of the community having heart attacks. Muslim youth need to meet, so they can eventually marry each other and raise Muslim kids. Otherwise, Muslim youth will marry non-Muslims, whom they can see and meet at the mall and other public places. Intermarriage will soar, and this book will be useless because a decent-sized American Muslim population won't exist. Full-time Islamic schools really are key to our future.

── 8 ◆ Muslims and American Politics: Creating Unity from the Inside Out ──

The Ayatollah Khomeini once said, "Islam is politics or it is nothing." I don't know what he meant, but I know that for American Muslims the question is, what kind of politics? It is almost unreasonable to expect all Muslims to agree on anything considering their diversity, ethnic and political. Diversity is not death in politics, but it makes issues more difficult to settle.

For example, African-Americans in the U.S. Congress have formed a group called the Congressional Black Caucus that discusses and forms a group opinion on political issues and policies having to do with African-Americans. This is a difficult task—attempting to speak for all African-Americans—considering how large and spread out that population is.

Now imagine a Congressional Muslim Caucus—this group's constituents would include African-Americans, South Asians, Central Asians, some Europeans, Native Americans, and white American converts among other ethnicities from a variety of economic backgrounds and nearly every state. Muslims, especially American Muslims, are not ethnically monolithic.

Compounding this diversity is the variety of political views within the community. Currently, American Muslims have paradoxical political views. Muslims are evenly divided between Republican and Democratic stances, as a group and individually. Muslims side with Democrats on several issues, from church/state separation and opposition to school prayer to pro-welfare and pro-affirmative-action stances.[1] At the same time,

Muslims also see value in Republican views, specifically pro-family Christian Coalition views like strict attitudes toward sex and alcohol consumption.[2] In addition, most Muslims of late probably prefer Republican foreign policy because Republicans have a history of being more understanding of Muslims abroad. What all Muslims do have in common is an Islamic basis for capitalist and democratic principles such as the right to own property and create and follow a constitution. These are themes Muhammad, a businessman himself, propagated. In fact, Muhammad is the author of one of the world's first constitutions written in his role as mediator for the town of Medina in 622 CE. The Medina Constitution espoused democratic principles, including recognition of rights for non-Muslims (specifically the Jews living in Medina).

I predict, however, despite this lack of unity, the Muslim vote, estimated at about 700,000 by American Muslim intellectual Dr. Aslam Abdullah, will be consequential in elections from 2000 onward. Abdullah says that Muslim votes could be the deciding factor in at least thirty-seven Congressional seats and even the Presidential Election in five key states with large Muslim populations. Both presidential candidates sent representatives to the largest annual gathering of American Muslims— the ISNA Convention over the 2000 Labor Day weekend. Even Tipper Gore and Hadassah Lieberman arrived unsolicited to stump for their husbands! Not one to be left out, Ralph Nader (actually of Arab descent though not Muslim) also attended. Dr. Abdullah points out that Walter Mondale turned down money from Muslims sixteen years ago, and now the Democratic candidates' wives are rubbing elbows with 30,000 American Muslims! For the first time, the Muslim vote is being taken seriously. It belongs to no party, putting it in the enviable position, for once, of being catered to.

The effects of American Muslim diversity are political disunity and an inability to influence political policy despite our size.

Though American Muslims may already outnumber Jews or will in the next five years, "Muslim influence on U.S. foreign policy continues to be only a fraction of that exercised by Jewish Americans," writes Ali Mazrui in his essay "Between the Crescent and the Star-Spangled Banner: American Muslims and U.S. Foreign Policy." Jews, unlike Muslims, have "strategically placed" themselves to influence U.S. policy. In addition, though Muslims are randomly politically active, they respond to policy making from four different identities: their national identity, their racial identity, their religious identity as Muslims, and as American immigrants (or as indigenous Americans).[3] American Jews seem to have reached a consensus on major issues while American Muslims are still trying to reconcile their various identities.

The most important and obvious point about Muslims' participation in American politics is the absence of a mainstream Muslim in a prominent political office. Muslims are as active in American politics as they can be *without* occupying office. They raise money for candidates and lobby for Muslim causes, but they rarely run for office. Though members of the Nation of Islam (NOI) have run for office, and Louis Farrakhan, leader of NOI, is a major political figure, the great majority of American Muslims do not feel they are represented by NOI. The NOI agenda of economic separatism for African-Americans and Farrakhan's racist and anti-Semitic speech seems un-Islamic to many, if not most, American Muslims.[4]

Many prominent Muslims involved in American politics see electing a Muslim congressperson as a major goal but do not run themselves. A few important factors seem to be keeping politically active Muslims from seeking office. First, the large conservative, immigrant-oriented element within the American Muslim population, despite the connections between Islam and democratic themes, dislikes the idea of a Muslim in Congress. Without this vocal group's support (and more likely with its dissension), Muslim candidates would face an uphill battle, not only in opposing well-known incumbents with large campaign budgets, but also from within their own community. Such support is necessary if a Muslim is to seek and serve in office.

In examining the cases of two former Muslim congressional candidates, Riaz Hussain of New York and Bill Quraishi of California, one sees the vehemence with which some conservative Muslims, particularly immigrant Muslims, believe in the separation of Muslims from American culture, including politics. Both candidates sought Muslims' votes, but conservative Islamic groups disliked the candidates' "accommodations to Western culture," specifically lack of beards, a Western name for Quraishi and so on. Hussain and Quraishi did not have these problems with more liberal Islamic organizations, organizations that currently make up the new Muslim lobby.[5] Like Hussain and Quraishi, the "emerging lobby has also fought Muslim attitudes, dating to the 1960s, that politics would corrupt the Muslim soul and identity." The Muslim lobby had to take the step of "leaving behind old suspicions about involvement in government" in order to have political influence in America, because conservatives' plans would be to stay out of politics and indirectly affect policy.[6] American Muslims want more influence than that.

Second, American Muslims tend to become jealous of those who have succeeded in leading the community and manifest their jealousy by not supporting that Muslim. The Muslim not acting thinks he or she would do a better job, criticizing activists for having the wrong ideas or wasting funds raised. This is true sometimes for all American-Islamic leadership positions. Who wants to lead a community that may be bitter and divided? Constant criticism of what hasn't been done for world and American Muslims would follow our Muslim Congressperson constantly.

Third, some Muslims may not run for office because they are disturbed by overwhelming U.S. policy against Muslims, especially the implicit lack of support for Palestinians, who are mostly Muslims, not to mention Kashmiris, Pakistanis, Chechnyans, Kosovars, and Bosnians. Confused over American inability to understand Muslims' suffering, many Muslims simply do not even vote.

However, Muslims have made significant progress on being recognized symbolically, perhaps more so than any other group in

the past few years. In the fall of 1995, Vice President Albert Gore
became the highest ranking U.S. official to visit a mosque. A few
months later, Hillary Rodham Clinton spoke in Los Angeles to a
group of Muslims, the first First Lady to address a gathering of
Muslims outside the White House. President Clinton's July 12,
1995, speech on religious freedom acknowledged Muslims several
times. African-American Muslim leaders Siraj Wahhaj and
Warith Deen Muhammad delivered invocations in the House and
Senate, respectively. Friday prayers are now held regularly in
the U.S. Capitol building for Muslim staffers, federal employees,
and other Muslims in the area. Since 1998, a crescent and star is
displayed on the White House lawn alongside a menorah and
Christmas tree, thanks to the tireless efforts of the late
Muhammed Mehdi of New York, who popularized the idea of
USA: Muslim Day, falling on the third Friday of December.
President George Bush began a tradition of wishing Muslims a
happy holiday on Eid, which President Clinton has expanded
upon by holding an Eid celebration in the White House, usually
attended by Ms. Clinton. In fact, American Muslims are indebted
to the Clintons for their embracing of Islam in the United States,
Islamic traditions, and visiting Islamic countries. The Clintons
have done more than any other First Family to raise the public
stature of Muslims, especially American Muslims, and to draw a
distinction between Muslim radicals and the beauty of true Islam
as practiced by 1.2 billion people. At the January 10, 2000, Eid al-
Fitr reception at the White House, President Clinton became the
first sitting president to meet with American Muslim leaders. He
said, "Too many Americans still know too little about Islam, now
practiced by one of every four people."[7]

Symbolic recognition is important because such actions, in
America, create a distinction, politically and socially, between
the majority of Muslims, who are mainstream, and the more controversial Muslims like Farrakhan of NOI and extremist groups.
Hopefully this symbolic recognition will lead to more political
recognition and influence.

Yet it seems that only wealthy Muslims are making an effort
to impact American politics. For example, attendance at Hillary

Clinton's speech in Los Angeles required a 300-dollar donation to the Muslim Public Affairs Council (MPAC), the group sponsoring the lecture. Muslims' political influence may be limited to Muslims like Niranjan Shah and Rashid Chaudary, who raised over 100,000 dollars for the Clinton-Gore reelection campaign and possibly more for the Democratic Party.[8] But we, as Muslims and Americans, should remind ourselves that, while donating is not wrong or bad, voting is the cheapest and the most democratic way to have influence. Every Muslim can and should vote.

Can American Muslims unify to influence American policy, and do they want to? How can we encourage all Muslims to vote? What effect will American Muslims have on American politics?

From what I've described, American Muslim political unification may seem impossible. Muslims run the gamut in political beliefs: pro-choice and pro-life, pro-death penalty and anti-death penalty, as well as undecided. How could we ever agree?

American Muslims have, unlike American Jews, made the mistake of defining ourselves politically by looking at issues external to our own community, like abortion and the death penalty, as mentioned. While it is important that all Americans learn about those issues and make informed decisions, it is equally imperative that American Muslims realize that such issues are not of the utmost concern to the white American convert to Islam living in Peoria or the immigrant Arab in Denver.

We should form our politics by looking *inside* our community and bringing our values *outward*. Instead, we form our political goals and values by looking to the *outside* to develop our *inside*, core values. There are a few matters that are very important that I can hardly imagine any American Muslim, even the conservative element, being against.

American Muslims' primary issue should be a push for greater understanding of Islam and Muslims among Americans. American Muslims should concentrate practically all their efforts on educating their fellow Americans. We should see our

Congressional representatives and tell them how many Muslims live in the country and in their state. We should give presentations on Islam in our children's schools. We should be active in community organizations and make ourselves available to speak as Muslims. We need to hold open houses at our mosques. We need to show Americans that we are here, and that we are not terrorists but good Americans. Specifically, the two Muslim holidays, Eid al-Udha and Eid al-Fitr should be recognized as holidays, at least at the local government level. Since 1997, the New York City Board of Education has recognized the right of Muslim students to celebrate the two holidays as legal holidays in the public schools.

The second objective is similar: U.S. adoption of friendlier, more understanding and tolerant diplomacy with Islamic countries and a real effort by policymakers to learn more about Islam. We know that a tremendous information gap regarding Islam exists among U.S. policymakers. Dr. Gasser Hathout, chairman of MPAC and prominent American Muslim, writes, "[F]ormer Defense Secretary Robert McNamara has stated that more understanding and engagement took place with the Soviet Union during the Cold War than with leaders of Islamic movements today."[9]

More American Muslims are frustrated by the suffering of Kashmiri Muslims at the hands of the Indian government, despotically occupying Kashmir's land in violation of U.N. guidelines, than by anything else. It would be rare to find an Islamic center that has not posted information on how to help Muslims who are victimized in Kashmir and other areas of conflict like Kosovo and Chechnya.

Accurately, Muslims see a double standard in American foreign policy.[10] The United States vigorously defeats Iraq in Desert Storm as mandated by U.N. resolutions and, at the same time, ignores equally important U.N. resolutions on Palestine, Bosnia, Chechnya, and Kashmir. The United States finally assists Muslims (the Kuwaitis), but only when a Muslim was the aggressor. In the other cases where Muslims are victims, American Muslims have concluded that the United States does not act strongly. Muslims believe the inaction is based on a belief in what is called the Islamic Threat, perceived to be, after the fall of Communism, the largest threat to democracy. Muslims see themselves as victimized and misunderstood in the world.[11] The world strains itself to empathize with the Israelis, the Indians, nearly everyone except Muslims.

Muslims tend to look to U.S.-Israel politics as a barometer or yardstick of their own political virility. Naturally, Muslims are often frustrated. While the majority of American Muslims readily accept Israel's existence and sovereighty as a nation, many wish for a prominence in society similar to that of American Jews. Muslims have a desire for parity. American Muslims also want some empathy for the situation of some world Muslims, especially Palestinians. For example, American Muslims would love it if some important politician would say, "It hasn't been easy for the Palestinians either, after all." Hillary Clinton once, before she changed her views, tried to express support for an eventual Palestinian homeland. As if to scare off Palestinian supporters from speaking their mind, Hillary was instantly pummeled by media and political analysts, saying that she should keep her opinions to herself. Would we have had the same reaction if she had said the opposite? I don't think American Muslims want to take anything away from Israel, but they would like to see Muslims treated better in the world and they would like to be proud that the United States led the way.

Third, American Muslims should stand for open immigration policies. A sizable number of American Muslims are here because of President Lyndon B. Johnson's immigration reform, ending country quotas favoring European émigrés and beginning a great wave of immigration from Islamic countries.

Fourth, American Muslims should condemn discrimination against Muslims in any form: vandalism of Islamic centers or a Muslim family's home to job discrimination directed against a Muslim woman based on her wearing *hijab.*

I know that practically all American Muslims would agree to at least these objectives. Other Muslims may have more suggestions, but this is a framework for us to build upon. I believe internal analysis is the key for us to succeed politically. When we take these four objectives to the Republican or Democratic convention and tell each group, "We will join whoever agrees with us," we can safely deliver a large number of Muslim votes, based on what we as a community feel is important, *not what American culture has deemed worthy of debate.*

We do have a large number of votes to deliver. According to an exit poll conducted by *Minaret* magazine and MPAC of 400 randomly selected Muslims, 65 percent of Muslims are registered to vote, and, of those registered, 76 percent voted in the 1996 general election. A *Minaret* magazine survey in the same year indicated that over two-thirds of American Muslim households participate in elections.[12] The Washington, D.C., based Council on American-Islamic Relations (CAIR) commissioned the John Zogby Group of New York to do a similar poll, which found that 68 percent of American Muslims are registered to vote.[13]

If these polls are accurate and representative, the goal of registering Muslims and encouraging Muslims to vote has been met. With well over half the registered population voting, Muslims vote more than Americans overall! These new Muslim political organizations and the strong voter turnout among Muslims creates a body that can influence American politics. If we implement a platform based on American Muslim concerns, from the inside out we could really have a chance at influencing American policy positively.

Much of the groundwork for being more influential has been laid. The American ethos of civic involvement has emboldened Muslims and encouraged them to take action at the grassroots level. Muslims even sent delegates to the party conventions: seven to the Republican and twenty-six to the Democratic. Both conventions featured an opening invocation by Muslim clergy— Talat Othman at the Republican and Maher Hathout at the Democratic.

Muslims have attempted to influence American domestic and foreign policy in several ways. They have protested legislation that they feel is unfairly biased against Muslims. For example, the American Muslim Council (AMC) played a large role in bringing about the defeat of a bill titled "The Freedom from Religious Persecution Act of 1997," which singled out Muslims as the chief aggressors in attacking minorities. AMC, ISNA, and MPAC also participated in the 1998 White House Conference on Hate Crimes.

They represent America abroad; Dr. Laila Al-Marayati, president of the American-based Muslim Women's League, was appointed by the White House to advise the U.S. United Nations delegation to the Beijing Conference on women. The AMC, in alliance with TransAfrica, played a large role in bringing sanctions against South Africa in protest of apartheid.[14] In fact, Muslims have been involved in influencing almost every aspect of American life, from instituting all-female swimming classes in public schools in order to protect female modesty to selecting candidates for local and national office who are sympathetic to Muslim causes.

The Muslim Public Affairs Council (MPAC) organized a highly successful children's rally against going to war with Iraq in March 1998. Besides co-sponsorship by the All Saints Church of Pasadena and the Wilshire Temple, the event was covered by the *Los Angeles Times* and the Central News Network (CNN). MPAC was very creative in holding a rally that presented American children of varying religious backgrounds speaking out against going to war with Iraq on behalf of Iraqi children and the children of the rest of the world. MPAC's allying with like-minded groups and focusing on Iraq really paid off, as I believe the millions who saw a video of the rally on CNN were quite moved.

The AMC coordinates lobbying and other actions from its Washington, D.C., headquarters, while the Los Angeles-based MPAC sees itself as "a public service agency which strives to make Islamic ethical values available to the American political process."[15] The American Muslim Alliance (AMA), based in

California, organizes political events, such as conferences between politicians and Muslim leaders. AMC, MPAC, and AMA want to make the Muslims of America more influential, a goal they share with the numerous Muslim political action committees (PACs). These organizations are becoming more influential by establishing themselves as authorities for members of Congress and the media to consult.

Beyond implementing the inside-out platform on an individual level and through the organizations that make up the new Muslim lobby, gaining political influence will be a slow process, perhaps involving just one person at a time.

A Muslim member of the Clinton/Gore reelection campaign, Mona Mohib, convinced campaign staff members to answer Muslims' questions directly by printing answers in a popular North American Muslim magazine, the *Minaret*. The Republican ticket, the Dole/Kemp campaign, instead of answering questions prepared by the *Minaret,* sent a previously prepared statement addressed to Muslims in reply to the magazine's request.[16] As more Muslims attain positions like Mona Mohib's, Muslim influence will grow.

In 1991, Charles Bilal, an African-American Muslim, was elected mayor of predominately white and non-Muslim Kountze, Texas, becoming the first Muslim mayor of an American city. Another Muslim, Adam Shakoor, served as deputy mayor of Detroit, which has a large Muslim community, in the early 90s.

In addition, Muslims have tried to become players in state and national political arenas. In 1994, Muslim political organizations endorsed seventy-seven gubernatorial and congressional candidates and, in 1996, ambitiously hoped to exchange endorsement of a presidential candidate for the appointment of a Muslim to a high administrative post.[17] Overwhelming endorsement of and contribution to Tim Johnson, challenger to South Dakota Senator Larry Pressler, probably contributed to Johnson's victory. Pressler probably didn't realize that Pakistanis and other Muslims would react so strongly to his "Pressler Amendment" which specified "Pakistan as a country working against U.S. interests in the region."[18]

American Muslims' action plan should have as its first step, unifying on an inside-out platform. I think we can unify nationally if we focus on what we agree on and let the rest of America argue over issues like bi-lingual education. We can leave the intricate discussions on Islam to families and mosques. Many immigrant Muslim leaders already are moving past a focus on foreign affairs to domestic issues and encouraging others to do the same. Salam Al-Marayati, director of MPAC, worked with other Muslims to put together a domestic political agenda for the elections since 1996 that addressed such topics as spousal abuse, parental rights, gang violence, abortion, euthanasia, and social spending.[19]

American Muslims have the opportunity to serve as models for Muslims of the world. It is likely that a mainstream American Muslim will be elected to national office some time in America's future. However, that Muslim will have to resolve himself or herself to having a multi-faceted identity within a diverse and somewhat divided community, especially if we continue to define ourselves politically from the outside in.

Will American Muslims need an event like the bus boycott in Montgomery, Alabama in order to unify, to see what we have in common? We can't count on that. We should all take off our holidays—Eid al-Udha and Eid al-Fitr—until they are recognized as official holidays. Like African-Americans did for Martin Luther King's birthday, we should stage a quiet protest against working and going to school on our important days for community-building until recognized.[20] We should realize what we can teach Americans—greater understanding, tolerance, acceptance—by being unified.

CLOSE-UP
Mahmoud Abdul Rauf, the American Flag, and Islam

In one of the few times Islam made the nightly news it was *not about* Islamic fundamentalist terrorists, but about a situation that made American Muslims look pretty bad anyway. Mahmoud Abdul Rauf, then point guard for the basketball team the Denver Nuggets, had spent most of the season sitting out the National Anthem in the locker room. When the National Basketball Association (NBA) finally did question him about this (and the conspiracy theorist in me says the NBA chose to bring up this issue at a crucial point in the season for the Nuggets, who were then trying to qualify for the playoffs), a media frenzy was set off.

For good reason too. Rauf cited a variety of reasons for not wanting to stand for the National Anthem and salute the American flag, the most overlooked of which was that he felt it was un-Islamic for him to worship anything besides God. The media and others focused on his next statements—he also did not want to stand for the flag because it represented, to him, the racism of America, that had held African-Americans down. Suddenly, everyone was talking about freedom of speech and freedom of religion and what it meant to be a Muslim in America, an African-American Muslim. I was thrilled, to say the least! My friends and I tuned in to Peter Jennings, who was actually talking about how American Muslims feel about the United States. Religious freedom in America, particularly American Muslims' ability to exercise freedom of religion, was the topic on everyone's mind; the subject had its fifteen minutes of fame.

Though legal analysts thought Rauf's case was strong, both under the First Amendment and the employment law (as his contract with the NBA may have been unconstitutional in requiring that he stand for the National Anthem), many Americans were vexed that Rauf could call the flag racist yet receive a salary of hundreds of thousands of American dollars with no qualms. "If we're such a racist country," people must have thought, "then don't take our money!" Veterans were mad that Rauf didn't see the flag as representing the battles for freedom America has participated in, making the debacle reminiscent of another African-American Muslim athlete's objections to American policy. World Champion boxer Muhammad Ali was arrested for refusing to comply with the draft for Vietnam, citing his Islamic beliefs and conscientious objector status.

I worried for a few minutes about the repercussions, especially on campus amongst my friends. Would people once and for all declare that Muslims are nuts? It's one thing to have a suicide Muslim bomber far away in another country. But here we were in the United States with a Muslim showing strong anti-American feeling. As a fellow Muslim and a fan, I wanted to support Rauf in the way that you want to support your brother or sister to those outside your family, even if you know they are wrong. I also knew that I never had a problem, as a Muslim, with standing for the flag and singing the National Anthem. I even remembered reading somewhere in the Qur'an that a good Muslim will follow the laws of his country because that is what God would want. I thought of Jesus' saying "Render unto Caesar what is Caesar's, and unto God what is God's."

I was confused reading my school's computer bulletin, where students had already delved into the topic. I had prepared myself for the worst. My fellow students were probably going to say something mean about American Muslims being no better than the horrid world Muslims. Imagine my shock when I read opinions from students of all sorts of backgrounds saying they thought Rauf had the right, as an American citizen, not to stand for the flag or the National Anthem. Some even said they empathized with Rauf's image of the flag as waving in the background of a lynching of African-Americans after the Civil War. Though it was far from a Rauf love fest, I was again surprised by my fellow Americans' ability to understand other opinions. "I'm with Mahmoud on this," wrote my friend Simi on Wellesley's Pro-Sports computer bulletin, citing his constitutional right to freedom of expression.

What American Muslims had trouble with was Rauf's inter-pretation of Islam. I would say many other American Muslims believe in the American flag as representative of Americans' struggle (you could even say Americans' *jihad*) for freedom and democracy in personal lives and around the world. Other Muslim athletes like Kareem Abdul-Jabar called Rauf, as did American Muslim leaders, and eventually persuaded him to stand during the Anthem, while he said an Islamic prayer to himself. That way, he was not being pulled away from focusing on Allah by singing to the flag.

From a national perspective, you could say that the Rauf sit-uation was a public relations disaster for Muslims. While other events involving negative acts perpetrated by Muslims could be explained, here was one of our own, an African-American convert to Islam, making us look bad. When I'm feeling down anyway about Americans' image of Muslims, I think that way. In truth though, I think American Muslims actually came out on top in the end.

For about two days, our friends, neighbors, and colleagues asked us questions about Islam. They wanted to know if it really was against our religion to stand for the flag. We had an oppor-tunity to talk to our fellow Americans about what Islam is and what being a Muslim means.

I tried to make good use of our time by talking about Islam and Qur'anic interpretation in a political science seminar I was taking. The group of about twenty students all had questions for me, as they all knew I was Muslim. Our class met once a week, so by the time we met, about a week after the incident, the situ-ation had been resolved. I nevertheless brought up the event dur-ing the beginning of class when we talked about current events. My classmates could tell I was excited, and they took advantage of my openness to ask questions: "Is it blasphemous in Islam to stand for the American flag? Have you ever refused to stand for the flag?"

I told them that it is written in the Qur'an that we must all read the Qur'an for ourselves and interpret what each passage means for ourselves. If our interpretation was wrong or if we felt someone else's was wrong, we are supposed to let God deal with that on Judgment Day. "That's why I can't say that Mahmoud Rauf is being a bad Muslim," I told the class. "It's between him and God." I explained that I had no problem standing for the flag but could see Rauf's point that, in Islam, one is not supposed to worship anyone or anything besides God and that standing for the flag may amount to such worship for someone who is really devout. I added, though, that the Qur'an instructs Muslims to respect their country's laws, and, if they can't do that as Muslims, they should move. "I don't think he's trying to be a troublemaker. I think he really feels that way." Other students compared the situation to that for members of the Jehovah's Witness faith who are protected by the Constitution in not standing for the flag under freedom of religion stipulated in the First Amendment.

An older woman in our class, a nontraditionally aged student who had come back to school, asked me, "Is there anything that would offend a Muslim as much not standing for the American flag offends some Americans?" I thought about that for a minute, and then said, "If someone went into a mosque during prayer time and disrupted the prayer session, that would be seriously offensive to Muslims." The class took this information in. They were interested in that answer.

When we met again a week later, we all let out a little nervous laughter in revisiting the topic. Because by now, a week later, two Denver radio station disc jockeys had done just what I had said: they had disrupted prayers at the Denver mosque by blasting music. It was as if someone had overheard our conversation and had been looking for something that would even the score against Muslims. Though the DJs' acts were humiliating for American Muslims, Muslims did not lash out at the radio station. Mosque representatives, as they had politely asked the DJs to leave the mosque, also gracefully pursued their grievances with the radio station. Much good came out of the event in the end, with the radio station agreeing to apologize publicly for a period of time, to conduct seminars on Islam for their employees, and to set up an internship program for Muslim college students interested in going into broadcasting. Besides that though, my political science class bonded over this issue and learned more about each other. In many ways, though the perception of Islam by some may have become more negative, I'm glad Rauf, who will now be playing for the Vancouver Grizzlies, challenged the NBA on standing for the flag. Not because I agree with what he did but because it gave Americans the chance to talk about Islam and the role of religion in America.

—— *9* ◆ Sizzling Sex . . . and Bacon ——

My sister likes to tell a story about a Columbia University Muslim student group *iftaar* (the prayer and meal held after a day of fasting during Ramadan) she attended when she was a student at Barnard College. She had stunned the conservative, young Muslim crowd by breaking the norm of gender segregation and sitting at the same table with a male Moroccan student she knew. The rest of the group gaped at her as the two chatted. She says now that she wished she had been even bolder and placed her hand on his shoulder—what horror that would have caused!

The students stared at them because normally in gatherings, as I've said, Muslims divide up by gender. Some argue there is a Qur'anic basis for this—partially to preserve women's modesty. However, from my perspective, such interpretations are quite literal, to a fault even, and do not take into account that we live in America, where men and women freely mingle. So my sister did it—she just sat and ate her meal with him. "We might as well have been having sex for the looks we got!" Aliya says. They just stared with their mouths hanging open. When Aliya shared a bagel with her friend, the rest of the group may have suffered cardiac problems.

Such segregation is usually the result of carrying over cultural traditions from one's native country. In Pakistan and other Islamic countries, the local mosque is merely a place to pray; that was particularly true at the time when today's immigrants to America lived there. Women stayed home to watch the children and attend to home affairs. The Qur'an actually excuses women

166

from praying at a mosque for that reason—to watch her children and the house. The mosque in these countries, though, is different from an American mosque in an important way that behooves the equal inclusion of women. Mosques in America have been shaped in response to the model of American churches and synagogues: a place of worship as a community center for the group as well, where members of the faith can socialize and meet each other. Since my mosque is a community center and not merely a place to pray, I want to feel respected, not resentful. I want to feel that I am a part of the community. Many American mosques point to the fact that they have a women's board of directors which assists the usually all-male board of directors that oversees all the mosque activities. To me it is yet another separation.

The absurdity of carrying over this mostly cultural tradition to the United States is evident in the friction Muslims like me and my sister who grew up here feel with this segregation. We're Americans, and *Brown v. Board of Education* might as well be stamped on our foreheads: separate is inherently unequal and confers a badge of inferiority on the group that is separated. Women in Islam are not inferior. To separate them implies so. I'm tired of going to mosques and being told: "Sisters pray upstairs/in the basement/in the side rooms," areas that are inevitably inferior in some respect, either having no heating or being too far away from the main prayer room to actually hear the imam's *khutba*. Mothers are usually expected to take their children, both boys and girls, with them, to the sisters' area. As a result, the sisters' prayer area usually resembles an out-of-control day care center. It's not easy to concentrate on praying. The balconies eerily remind me of the segregation the African-American community suffered through, as they were forced to sit in crowded balconies in churches, courtrooms and movie theaters, though of course the African-American community suffered much more than American Muslim women do.

I don't see why we can't all pray in the same room, split by gender down the middle of the room. If we are to be judged by God on Judgment Day with no distinction considered other than our piety, why can't we pray in the same room? If men and women pray alongside each other in Mecca, why can't we in our local mosque? If we are split down the middle, women and men don't have to worry about prostrating in front of a person of the opposite sex, a potentially embarassing situation. Yet we can enjoy sharing prayer to God together, in one unified group, in one room. Muslims shall stand before God on Judgment Day like this in a mixed gender group.

When I tell this to men who defend separating women, they think I'm only trying to cause trouble. But this is really about respect. I want to know that I'm respected in my mosque and received as a peer, an equal. I do see the benefits of separation in some situations, but at the mosque, our community center, I want to feel included, not excluded. Special protections are sometimes tantamount to the protectors' saying, "You *need* to be protected because you're weak and can't do it yourself." Well let *me* watch out for *myself,* and you worry about yourself.

My uncle Adnan says that having women alongside while he prays would be distracting. He just wants to concentrate on God at this time, but he says, instead, he would be thinking about that girl near him praying. As with *hijab,* I feel that women are expected to modify *their* behavior because men say they have inadequacies and cannot control themselves. I can respect wanting to concentrate on God, but it's hard for the women to concentrate if we're freezing or if our kids are running around hitting each other. There is no Qur'anic basis for this distraction theory, and, no disrespect to my uncle, it sounds too much like men making excuses to preserve their space.

The effect of this separation is amazing. To the point where my brother jokes that films of men and women merely dining together are considered racy, pornographic material in Arab countries, where the segregation is even more stringent because of non-Islamic, cultural influences. Imagine Arab teenage boys passing around *Samire Does Dubai.* One says to the another, "In this one, she sits at a table *with two guys!* They all share one plate of spaghetti!"

I may make myself unwelcome at many mosques in the United States, but I really think men just want to protect their big prayer rooms where they can line up behind the mosque religious leader, the *imam*. Maybe they enjoy knowing we're sitting somewhere else, a position of shame in the basement as opposed to a position of honor behind the *imam*. It's just patriarchy. The reasons to preserve segregation are not good ones. I'm tired of Muslim women having to make concessions, like sitting somewhere else instead of the position of honor, or wearing *hijab* because men can't control themselves. We serve the punishment for a man's insecurity over not acting on temptation. If I'm wrong about this, I would love for a male member of a mosque with a similar division to invite me to sit with the men in the large prayer hall, and all the other sisters too.

My mom says that whenever there is segregation at a party, she inevitably ends up on the men's side by invitation—debating politics, exchanging jokes. I usually don't follow her, and I end up peeking over the partition to see what the men are doing. The partition actually raises my curiousity. If we are a community, let's be one and sit together. There is nothing in the Qur'an that solidly justifies such segregation. There is much in our native cultures that does, and we must move beyond that. We're Americans now, and Muslims, and must come together as such.

I could tell my life story based on my experiences with pork products. As a Muslim, I do not eat pork. In fact, the Qur'an lists a specific set of prescriptions for food and eating within Islamic guidelines, described by the term *halal*. These prescriptions are slightly less strict than and quite similar to the ones set down in the Torah, and the terms *halal* and *kosher* are practically interchangeable. The only part of the *halal* diet that I actually follow is the restriction on eating pork or any by-products produced from a pig. I don't think I'll be condemned on Judgment Day for not following a complete *halal* diet. I could be wrong about that, but, to me, there are other things that are more central to my identity as a Muslim, specifically contributing time and money to charitable causes and fasting during Ramadan.

When you live in a country where the majority of people eat pork freely, the Islamic restriction on pork ends up being really important. Anyone I have ever dined out with knows that I don't eat pork, and that's a lot of people! Let's say that, on the average, I've eaten out with various non-Muslims about once a week for the last ten years. Each of those 300 or so people heard me tell my waiter, "I can't eat pork. Could you make sure there isn't any in the food I ordered?" So whether I told my dining companion(s) that I don't eat pork because of religious reasons or if he or she intuited that on their own, many people know that I don't eat pork. These same people probably *don't know* that I fast during Ramadan or that I'm supposed to pray five times a day. What they know about Muslims through me is that we don't eat pork.

My parents taught me to follow this restriction on pork. To emphasize the point to my young brother, my mother told us that "pig" was a bad word, and we couldn't say it. As a result, we largely ignored Miss Piggy, focusing on other Muppets, and often spelled "pig" when we needed to use that word, saying, "Mom, is there p-i-g in this?" My brother was too young to know how to spell correctly and created his own innovation by saying, "I saw g-r-p's at the zoo!" We thought my brother's attempt at spelling pig was so funny that we adopted it and soon after were saying at restaurants, "We can't eat any g-r-p's" and, upon seeing our waiter's quizzical look added, "I mean, pork."

My parents continue to emphasize this restriction in all ways possible. One day I called home from boarding school to tell my mother I had a crush on a boy in my class. "Is he Christian?" my mom asked. "I guess," I responded, thinking that was far less important than that this boy and I were going to live happily ever after once he realized I existed. "Well," my mom stated in that motherly, matter of fact tone of hers, "I wouldn't want to kiss someone who's eaten pork! YUCK!" Clearly my mother's disapproval ended the relationship before it began. Other girls date boys who ride motorcycles to scare their mothers; I just have to date a boy who eats pork!

In the past few years, pork has enjoyed a revival in the culinary world, and I often find myself skipping over menu items that end with "wrapped in pork." I've also been dining out with friends a lot more in recent years. As a result, my dinner or lunch companion is treated to an unsolicited lesson on *halal* eating! Sometimes I ask the waiter if the item can be prepared without pork, and sometimes I just don't feel like going to the trouble and order another dish.

Not to be self-piteous, but I have to say that we Muslims and Jews who don't eat pork, and vegetarians, have it tough on this one. I'm assuming here that you, the reader, do not have religious conflicts with eating certain foods, are not a vegetarian, and do not have allergies to particular foods. Now imagine going to a restaurant and scanning the menu and not saying, "What am I in the mood for tonight?" You look at the menu and say, "What *can* I eat here?" Sometimes the choices are few, and, most of the time, it's not a problem. But I can honestly say that I've never had the luxury of ordering anything off the menu casually—I've always *analyzed* menus.

To tell you the truth, I didn't know I had it "worse off" until it was pointed out to me by a non-Muslim. The summer after my first year in college, I worked as an intern for U S WEST in Denver in the public relations department. I loved my job because my boss, a woman named Lisa Best, is a great person—funny, smart, motivating, and optimistic, she is everything you would want in a first boss. She gave me responsibility and expected me to perform, which I did happily.

One day, Ms. Best took our gang to lunch across the street at Le Peep, a restaurant that serves breakfast food all day. In those days, I didn't care about my weight and was really looking forward to a short stack of buttermilk pancakes with butter smeared all over them and moist brown syrup flowing down the sides like Niagara Falls. My family and I had eaten at Le Peep often so I wasn't worried about eating pork by mistake so long as I let our server know I didn't eat pork.

Once we ordered, I noticed that several others in our group were ordering pancakes with a side of bacon. So I specifically pointed out in my order that I absolutely could not have bacon anywhere in my order, just pancakes. The waitress seemed not to understand what I was saying, and Ms. Best emphasized the point. A few minutes later, the waitress brought out an order of pancakes with long brown and red strips of bacon, oozing grease and juice, lying at the pancakes' side, and placed it in front of me.

Similar incidents had happened to me before, and they are always awkward. I always wonder, as I see my server heading for me with a dish that has bacon in it, should I say something before he or she puts the plate down, or would that be rude? Usually I wait till they put the plate down, as I did at Le Peep, and I check the food to make sure I'm not seeing things. In the case of the pancakes, though they looked innocent enough themselves, that was definitely bacon there, at the stack's side.

"Oh, you know, I can't eat these," I said nicely. As I had learned, it was best to act surprised and sweet rather than shocked and disgusted. "I can't eat pork." Then recalling an associate who did order bacon on the side, I asked the server if she wanted to give this order to her.

"Well, hers is already being prepared. Why don't I just take the bacon off this one?" The waitress's hands moved towards my plate. "Well, you see, I can't eat these pancakes because the juices of the pancakes and bacon have already mixed, and I can't eat anything that's touched the bacon." The waitress held the plate in her hand now. I offered, "Why don't you just leave this plate here, and I'll just order another stack of pancakes?" That way I would know I was getting a new set of pancakes and not the same set with the bacon removed.

And then an argument ensued. The waitress defiantly shifted the plate of the illicit pancakes and bacon to her palm and moved it closer to her head: "I don't see why you can't eat it. It's all cooked on the same griddle!" I was speechless for a moment with this point. It is true that cooks can do whatever they want in the restaurant kitchen. For all I know they're washing their hands with lard. I replied, with enough meekness to keep a fight from breaking out, "I know that, but I'd just prefer to eat fresh pancakes."

Throughout this meal, I could feel Ms. Best's body tempera-
ture rise as she became more annoyed. No one appreciated the
waitress's attitude, but I was used to it. This had happened to me
before, and I was prepared to deal with it.

But Ms. Best was horrified that my original instructions had
been ignored and she had tried to say something before, but I had
managed to hold my own. My co-workers sat quietly with their
eyes peeled on me and the waitress, as if we were a soap opera.
The waitress started to say something, and Ms. Best burst out,
"Just leave that plate here with me, and go to the kitchen and get
plain pancakes!" The waitress started up again but before she
could get past, "But ———," Ms. Best ordered, "Just do it! Now!"

A silence came over the table. I don't think any of us had
seen Ms. Best that angry before. I remembered my manners and
said, "Thank you." I was surprised at how dramatic the event
had become. Ms. Best replied by saying how ridiculous it was
that the waitress didn't understand my initial request, that my
needs as a customer were ignored, and that the waitress must
have a problem with people who follow dietary restrictions or
have a hearing problem or something. As the rest of the group
envisioned the waitress's tip diminishing, I suddenly realized
what I had been taking for granted: I had always accepted being
mistreated at restaurants because of my special request of no
bacon. It took Ms. Best, a non-Muslim, to make me realize that I
deserved to have my religious beliefs respected.

Ms. Best calmed down, after complaining that we shouldn't
be charged for my dish due to the server's mishandling, and we
all ate well. But after that lunch, I knew that I would never order
at restaurants apologetically again. I am a Muslim after all, and
there is nothing wrong with my requesting no pork. That's what
being an American is all about—being able to say, I don't want to
do this because it compromises my religious beliefs. Who would
have thought empowerment could come from ordering lunch at a
breakfast-theme restaurant?

I admit that, in today's world, especially in first-world countries, there is no good reason *not* to eat pork. According to historical sources, Muhammad instructed his followers not to eat pork

because pork was often cooked improperly, and many died from consequent bacterial complications. Today, we rarely encounter that problem, but practically all Muslims continue to follow the restriction on pork. When I tell my server at a restaurant that I can't eat pork, I'm sometimes tempted to say I'm allergic to it, and sometimes I do. Servers instantly understand and become vigilant. It's unfortunate that we can't understand religious beliefs in the same way. While there is no scientific reason not to eat pork, other than to cut down on fatty foods and calories, observing the restriction keeps me close to the Prophet Muhammad and reminds me that I am a Muslim. It is a tradition that ties me to the Muslims of the world and the Muslims of past history.

That may seem silly, that I feel a cultural and historical bond when I refrain from eating pork. But all cultures have their ways of remembering their past and bringing the community together. Suppose the U.S. Congress were to create a commission whose sole task was to issue laws that would make Americans' lives easier. Sounds good, right? And one of the laws they issue is a ban of the observance of Thanksgiving. In the opinion of the commission's chairman, "Thanksgiving compels Americans to spend more money and effort on food, food preparation, and travel in order to commemorate an event that by most historical accounts did not happen."

Wait a second though! As an American, I love Thanksgiving. It is a day set aside to be thankful for our blessings, as free persons living in the United States, and to honor the pioneering spirit of the Pilgrims, whether they actually had a Thanksgiving dinner or not, and the American spirit of cooperation, as perceived to have occurred between the Pilgrims and Native Americans. It may seem silly to a person from France or Syria, and I wouldn't expect them to celebrate Thanksgiving, but I do expect them to accept it and even try to understand it a little. I feel the same way about eating *halal.* I don't expect every American to give up pork, but I do expect them to respect my beliefs.

10 ✦ Where American Islam Is Going

A few years ago, my mother mentioned something about how nice two of the Jewish families in our hometown, Pueblo, Colorado, had been when we first moved there. My mom thought maybe it had something to do with the fact that these families had known what it was like to be non-Christian in a Christian town. "You know," she said, "the Pueblo Country Club had only started accepting Jews as members a few years before we moved." I was shocked to hear this! I had no idea that our modest, local country club had ever, in its history, not accepted anyone. We had moved to Pueblo around 1975—I couldn't even imagine that up until the early seventies, Jews had been excluded at country clubs. These friends of ours are among Pueblo's most social families; one of them even writes the social column in our local newspaper.

It then occurred to me that Muslims could have been excluded from the country club, too. So I asked my mom if the club ever attempted to exclude us, as Muslims. She replied, with a laugh, "Nobody here knew enough about Muslims to leave us out!" That's one time I was happy about American ignorance of Islam.

As a group, American Muslims face an uncertain, yet hopeful, future. The most popular and obvious possibility is that American Muslims will assimilate into American society, in a way that other religious groups have done.

What I see is Muslims who attend mosque services and have Islamic values, but at extended levels are part of American society, bringing their knowledge of Islam with them. I envision American Muslim families in communities all over America, who

175

have both non-Muslim and Muslim friends and neighbors. I envision their children marrying other Muslims, some of whom may be converts and also of different ethnic origins. Some families will send their children to full-time Islamic schools, and some will not.

They will have their own identity, not as Muslims or as Americans but *as American Muslims.*

American society will benefit from the added dialogue provided by Muslims. Muslims will benefit by reaching a dynamic in which they are a part of American society while maintaining an Islamic identity, their symbols and public observances melded into layers of American society and culture. In this scenario, Islamic holidays will be recognized, with many Muslim and non-Muslim Americans enjoying days off from work and school in celebration. Already, Syracuse University has become the first American educational institution to close on Eid al-Fitr.

Islam is a part of the religious foundation of Western culture. American Muslims, as Muslims living in the West, are rediscovering Islamic emphasis on what we recognize as Western ideas—tolerance, democracy, compassion—ideas cited in the Qur'an that have been unintentionally buried by centuries of Islamic scholarship and the practices of Eastern Muslim societies.

It is an exciting time to be an American Muslim. We stand at the threshold of redefining a centuries-old religion and carrying on Muslims' legacy of achievement. American freedom of thought, and separation from cultural amplifications of religious practice, are allowing American Muslims to adopt a leaner, more accurate Islam. This Qur'anic Islam is very compatible with Western lifestyle, as the vestiges of non-Western culture are dropped.

I call this re-discovery of Islam by American and Western Muslims the second Golden Age of Islam. The first Golden Age was so characterized because Islam flourished: Islam spread throughout the globe from the seventh century onward, and Muslims were the foremost scholars and thinkers of the world. The Muslims of history contributed to civilization in a number of ways: in algebra and geometry, with the creation of the number zero, in modern navigation, and architectural design, among many other advances. I predict that the second Golden Age of Islam will be so designated for primarily two reasons: because of the inner growth and strengthening of faith of Western Muslims *and* the successful adaptation of those Muslims to Western life without compromising their beliefs.

This Golden Age of Islam will occur primarily in the United States because Muslims in America are more comfortable than in other Western nations. Americans are not strongly anti-Islamic, as some English and French are, and, in America, Muslims are assured freedom of thought and practice under the First Amendment.[1] This freedom will lead to greater participation in, and therefore greater influence on, American society.

In America, where Islam can flourish without the restraints of culture and politics, Islam will no longer be equated with conflict and foreign lands, but will come to be identified with the familiarity of Muslim neighbors, classmates, and fellow carpool parents. Muslims will bring stability to their communities. Muslim businesses will create jobs, and families will commit to improving their neighborhoods and schools. Muslim families are strong; parents and children interact. The majority of Muslim children do not use drugs, drink alcohol, or engage in pre-marital sex providing, therefore, "positive peer pressure" on other kids their age. For these reasons, many of the negative myths about Muslims will be dispelled.

To create this second Golden Age of Islam, the American Muslim community must unify. In fact, one of the significant *jihads* or struggles that American Muslims are facing is unifying their community. Unification will take some time to achieve. While observers agree that the American Muslim community is coming together, groups do emerge that pose a challenge to overall unity.

A challenge may be presented by a growth of American Muslims who altogether cease practicing Islam. We can expect some abandonment of Islam among American Muslims, as has been noted in France.[2] It is important to stress, however, that, in America, the number of Muslims who subscribe to the Five

Pillars, including Eid Muslims, will outnumber those who become agnostics or even atheists. We will come to realize the presence of these "outside the flock" Muslims though, these minorities within a minority, as American Islam grows.

I often meet Christians or Jews who, although raised Catholic or Jewish, do not feel strongly about their religion outside of attending major religious ceremonies on Christmas or Rosh Hashanah. Acknowledging their upbringing, they sometimes say they are culturally, as opposed to religiously, Christian or Jewish. Similarly, we will start meeting more Muslims who identify themselves as culturally Muslim, in that they were raised Muslim and attend mosque services on major holidays, but they don't pray five times a day or expect women to cover their heads.

Some scholars already have noted this American Muslim group, calling them "Eid Muslims," who attend mosque on the two major Muslim holidays only. As long as Eid Muslims subscribe to the Five Pillars, the basic beliefs of Islam, and strict Muslims do not judge Eid Muslims harshly, Eid Muslims represent only a small challenge to unity.

Over thirty years ago, Muhammad Ali refused to fight in Vietnam. At that time, he was a very enigmatic character—a charismatic boxer who had chosen an odd religion. Today, Ali, a Sunni Muslim, is heralded by many Americans as a hero, an inspiration. Muhammad Ali is but one example of how dynamic the American Muslim community is. They are a thoughtful group that brings faith, honesty, and strong principles to modern America.

How will contemporary American Muslims be remembered? American Muslims' arrival as a national force will be defined by their *presence in society,* particularly as trained professionals. Tolerance will be an American-Islamic hallmark, exemplified by the various political organizations formed, the women's shelters created, the Islamic schools and ventures for social improvement with other like-minded groups. If you are expecting American Muslims, as their numbers increase, to rally around one particular issue, you likely will be disappointed. Muslims as a community do feel strongly on certain issues such as American support for Bosnian Muslims. However, as American Muslims unify, it will be primarily to draw support from each other and present a cohesive, positive image to other Americans.

American Muslims will demystify Islam for other Americans, no easy task, by interacting with them daily. For the most part, American Muslims are and will be just like other Americans—concerned with their families, with improvement of their communities, with schools and standards of living. In essence, American Muslims will be known for being American, having the same worries and needs their neighbors have. While this may seem rather unmonumental, it is not. Teaching Americans and the West about Islam, creating a better understanding of it, will be American Muslims' contribution and legacy to the world as they combine the best of American culture with the best of Islam.

CLOSE-UP
A Direct Relationship with God

When a Muslim prays, it is between him or her and God; there are no clergy that must conduct the relationship. Though it is believed to be better to pray in groups, a Muslim can pray alone. So, while rabbis in Judaism and the Pope in Catholicism make interpretations of their holy books that are binding on those who follow them, Muslim ministers cannot do so. In Islam, individuals must read the Qur'an themselves and interpret. God will deal with them and their interpretations on Judgment Day. It is not the place of a Muslim to tell another that he or she has sinned against God; Muslims believe that only God can make such a pronouncement.

NOTES

Close-Up: Islam and Slavery in Early American History: The *Roots* Story

1. Alex Haley, *Roots* (New York: Dell Publishing, 1977), 65.
2. Ibid., 153.
3. Ibid., 71.
4. Clyde-Ahmad Winters, "Afro-American Muslims—From Slavery to Freedom," *Message*, March 1998: 19.
5. Muslim researcher Fareed H. Nu'man cites an 1178 Chinese document entitled the "Sung Document" recording the voyage of Muslim sailors to a land known as Mu-Lan-Pi, understood to mean the Americas, possibly North America. The Sung Document is later referenced in a 1933 publication entitled *The Khotan Amirs* (see Fareed H. Nu'man, *The Muslim Population in the United States: A Brief Statement* [Washington, D.C.: American Muslim Council, 1992], 19–20). If Nu'man's research is correct, and there is no reason to believe it is not, Muslims explored America 300 years before Columbus discovered America. The journeys of Abu Bakari, a Muslim explorer and king of the Malian Empire, in 1310 to the New World are well known. Other Muslim explorers from Mali and other West African countries, according to Nu'man, arrived at the Gulf of Mexico in 1312 to explore the American interior using the Mississippi River as an access route. The same waters that now host Southern gambling ships once carried the earliest American Muslims and visitors! Jane Smith writes in her recent book, *Islam in America* (New York: Columbia University Press, 1999): "[S]ome scholars currently argue that for nearly two centuries before the time of Christopher Columbus's venture in 1492, Muslims sailed from Spain and parts of the northwestern coast of Africa to both South and North America and were among the members of Columbus's own crew" (50). She also writes that African Muslim explorers are believed to have moved deep into the continent, associating with Native Americans, even to the extent of introducing certain arts and crafts and intermarriage. Evidence, based on eyewitness accounts, artifacts, and inscriptions, neither confirms nor

discredits the possibility that some of the earliest Americans were Muslim. Even if Muslims do not receive credit for discovering America, they are believed to have been relied upon by Columbus for their navigation skills. In fact, Arab Muslims preserved the knowledge gathered by the early Greeks and Romans in the Middle Ages, facilitating the technological advances the Arab Muslims achieved in general and navigatory science (see Mary H. Cooper, "Muslims in America," *CQ Researcher*, 30 April 1993: 369). The Muslims of Spain, permanently expelled by Fernando and Isabella from Spain, also in 1492, with the capture of the last Muslim Spanish city, Granada, may have made it to Southern parts of the United States (Smith, *Islam in America*, 51). Nu'man says that Moors are recorded as living in South Carolina and Florida in 1790 (*The Muslim Population in the United States*, 20). We may never have solid scientific proof of the existence of early American Muslims, but even the theory that Muslims played a role in early American history thrills me! I feel the spirits of these early American Muslims today, manifesting itself in the few quiet yet intriguing conversions of Hispanic and Native American peoples to Islam today. Islam in America is at once possibly both our past and our future as Americans, and Islam in America is certainly part of our present existence in America today.

6. Yvonne Y. Haddad, *A Century of Islam in America* (Washington, D.C. The Middle East Institute, 1986), 1; Abdullah Hakim Quick, "Islam and the African in America: the Sunni Experience," *Message*, July 1997: 22..

7. Quick, "Islam and the African in America: the Sunni Experience," 22; Richard Wormser, *American Islam: Growing Up Muslim in America* (New York: Walker and Company, 1994), 71; Nu'man, *The Muslim Population in the United States*, 20.

8. Jeffrey Sheler, "Black Muslims: From Fringe to Bedrock," *U.S. News & World Report*, 8 October 1990: 71; Mary H. Cooper, "Muslims in America," *CQ Researcher*, 30 April 1993: 370; Karen N. Peart, "Converts to the Faith," *Scholastic Update*, 22 October 1993, teacher's ed.: 17.

9. Bilaal S. Abdullah, "African History and Emancipation: An Islamic Perspective," *Message*, March 1998: 14.

10. For more details on the topic of Africans in Islamic history, refer to Mr. Bilal Abdullah's article in the previous note.

11. Fazlur Rahman, *Major Themes of the Qur'an* (Minneapolis: Bibliotheca Islamica, 1989), 48.

12. "Dr. Mazuri speaks at Message Forum," *Message*, November/December 1996: 12.

Close-Up: The Sects of Islam

1. Mary H. Cooper, "Muslims in America," *CQ Researcher*, 30 April 1993: 370.
2. The major difference between the two sects is a disagreement on Prophet Muhammad's successor. For more information on Shi'ism, see also Allamah Sayyid Muhammad Husayn Tabatabai, *Shi'ite Islam*, trans. Seyyed Hossein Nasr (Albany: SUNY Press, 1975).

Chapter 2: The American Muslim

1. We don't know the exact number of Muslims in America for a few reasons. First, religious affiliation is not asked about on the U.S. Census due to separation of church and state. Second, we can only base our estimates on a few figures: mosque attendance, immigration from Islamic countries, and statistics compiled by American Islamic organizations. Most scholars agree that four to six million is a conservative and reasonable estimate of the American Muslim population and that American Muslims outnumber American Episcopalians. Some American Muslim organizations estimate that up to as many as nine to eleven million Muslims are living in the United States. In addition, most scholars agree that American Muslims will soon outnumber American Jews. There also seems to be agreement that the number of mosques is 2000 and Islamic schools are 200.

Close-Up: *Hijab* and the Single Girl: Will Men Ever Learn to Control Themselves?

1. Laurie Goodstein, "Scarves as a Dilemma to Muslims," *Denver Post*, 6 November 1997: 37A.

2. Aminah Beverly McCloud, *African-American Islam* (New York: Routledge, 1995), 183, 159.

3. Carol L. Anway, *Daughters of Another Path* (Lee's Summit, Mo.: Yawna Publications, 1996), 78.

4. Mary H. Cooper, "Muslims in America," *CQ Researcher*, 30 April 1993: 367.

5. "Muslim Woman Ticketed for Disguise," *Christian Century*, 26 October 1994: 979. Ten states have passed amendments to their anti-mask statutes which provide for religious exceptions; see Karima Al-Amin and Maisah Robinson, "Modesty Under Attack: Challenging 'Anti-mask' Statutes," *Message*, June 1997: 27–28, and "Muslim women win rights in Georgia," *Islamic Horizons*, March/April 1998: 9. A Virginia jury awarded two Muslim women $125,000 each who were arrested under the state's Anti-Mask statute. "Jury sides with Muslim Women Arrested while Wearing Veils," *Message*, November 1999: 9.

6. Council on American-Islamic Relations, *Press Release: Sears and Pinkerton Apologize for Firing / Sending Home Muslim Women Who Refused to Refuse Their Hijab* (Washington, D.C.: Council on American-Islamic Relations, 1995). See Abu Ali Bafaquih, "Muslim American Power Emerges," *Islamic Horizons*, November/December 1999: 26–28; Abu Amal Hadhrami, "Muslims Gain Political Rights," *Islamic Horizons*, January/February 1999: 24-25; "American Muslims continue gains," *Islamic Horizons*, November/December 1998: 10.

7. Goodstein, "Scarves a Dilemma to Muslims," 37A.

8. Kathy Dobie, "Women Lift Veil of Faith: Muslims Break Stereotypes," *Washington Post*, 22 June 1991: C6.

9. Muhammad Abdul-Rauf, "The Future of the Islamic Tradition in North America," *The Muslim Community in North America*, ed. Earle H. Waugh, Baha Abu-Laban, and Regula B. Qureshi (Edmonton: University of Alberta, 1983), 276.

10. Zehra Panjvani, "Women in Islam," Islamic Council of New England Conference, Durham, New Hampshire, 5 October 1996.

11. See also Anway, *Daughters of Another Path*, 75; Cooper, "Muslims in America," 373; Joan Sabree, "Masjid Felix Bilal: An Oasis in a Desert of Hopelessness," *Muslim Journal*, 2 June 1989: 7; and Oliver Michel, "Allah's G.I.'s," *World Press Review*, September 1992: 41.

12. Two articles by Robert Marquand in the *Christian Science Monitor* give an excellent overview of the issues surrounding *hijab*. I have

summarized them here: "Seriously Tinkering with 1,000 Years of Tradition," *Christian Science Monitor*, 12 February 1996: 1, 10–12; "The Hurricane That Swirls over the Head Scarf," *Christian Science Monitor*, 12 February 1996: 10–11.

13. Marquand, "Seriously Tinkering with 1,000 Years of Tradition," 11.
14. McCloud, *African-American Islam*, 143.
15. Marquand, "Seriously Tinkering with 1,000 Years of Tradition," 11.
16. "Women in Islam," Islamic Council of New England Conference, Durham, New Hampshire, 5 October, 1996.
17. Shahmim Ibrahim, personal interview, 14 August 1996; Najma Adam, personal interview, 21 September 1996.
18. Haddad and Lummis, *Islamic Values in the United States*, 133.
19. Marquand, "Seriously Tinkering with 1,000 Years of Tradition," 11.
20. Haddad and Lummis, *Islamic Values in the United States*, 126.
21. Najma Adam, personal interview, 21 September 1996.
22. "Muslim Feminist Hermeneutics," *In Our Own Voices: Four Centuries of American Women's Religious Writing*, ed. Rosemary Skinner Keller and Rosemary Radford Ruether (New York: Harper-SanFrancisco, 1995), 432–433.
23. Robert Marquand and Lamis Adoni, "Islamic Family Values Simmer in a U.S. Melting Pot," *Christian Science Monitor*, 29 January 1996: 1, 10–11.
24. Rasha El-Desuqi, "Women in Islam," Islamic Council of New England Conference, Durham, New Hampshire, 5 October 1996.
25. Susan Hill Lindley, *"You Have Stept Out of Your Place": A History of Women and Religion in America* (Louisville: Westminister John Knox Press, 1996), 421.
26. McCloud, *African-American Islam*, 109.
27. Smith, 240.
28. Marquand and Adoni, "Islamic Family Values Simmer in a U.S. Melting Pot," 11.
29. McCloud, *African-American Islam*, 146–147.
30. Haddad and Lummis, *Islamic Values in the United States*, 12; and Marquand, "The Hurricane That Swirls over the Head Scarf," 10–11.
31. Dobie, "Women Lift Veil of Faith," C7.
32. Anis Ahmed, personal interview, 17 January 1997.
33. "Voices of the Faithful," 18.
34. Anway, *Daughters of Another Path*, 79.
35. Dobie, "Women Lift Veil of Faith," C7.
36. Anway, *Daughters of Another Path*, 78.

37. Lindley, 420.
38. Anway, *Daughters of Another Path*, 168.
39. Ibid., 163.
40. Hayat Alvi, "Why Silicone Breast Implants?" *Message International*, May 1992: 33.
41. Dobie, "Women Lift the Veil of Faith," C6.
42. Anway, *Daughters of Another Path*, 75.
43. Dobie, "Women Lift the Veil of Faith," C7.
44. Anway, *Daughters of Another Path*, 166; and Haddad and Lummis, *Islamic Values in the United States*, 132–33.

Close-Up: We've Come a Long Way, Baby

1. Fareed H. Nu'man, *The Muslim Population in the United States: A Brief Statement* (Washington, D. C.: American Muslim Council, 1992), 15.
2. Steven Barboza, *American Jihad: Islam after Malcolm X* (New York: Image Books, 1994), 9.
3. Nu'man, *The Muslim Population in the United States,* 15.
4. For a full discussion of Islamic organizations in the United States, see Gutbi Mahdi Ahmed, "Muslim Organizations in the United States," in *The Muslims of America,* ed. Yvonne Yazbeck Haddad (New York: University Press, 1991), 11–24.

Close-Up: The Meaning of the Five Pillars of Islam

1. Julie Chao, "Pillar of Charity: Muslim Holy Month a Time for Charity," *San Francisco Examiner,* 31 December 1997: A1.

Chapter 4: Farrakhan's Choice: Militancy or Moderation

1. Sonsyrea Tate, *Little X: Growing Up in the Nation of Islam* (New York: HarperSanFrancisco, 1997), 33.

2. Ibid., 77.
3. Teresa Watanabe, "Healing a Bitter Legacy," *Los Angeles Times*, 8 July 2000: B2.
4. "The Family Grows," *Islamic Horizons*, March/April 2000: 10
5. Watanabe, "Healing a Bitter Legacy," B2.
6. Watanabe, "Healing a Bitter Legacy," B2; "U.S. Muslim Leaders Preaching Unity," *Chicago Tribune Wire Services*, 8 September 2000.
7. Malcolm X, Letter from Mecca to a friend, *New York Times*, 4 October 1964: 59.

Close-Up: In *Shahada*: Conversion and Renewal in Prison from Malcolm X to Mike Tyson

1. Jan Muhammad Diwan, personal interview, 6 April 1998. Abdul Raouf Nasir, personal interview, 10 February 1998.
2. Aslam Abdullah, "Ramadan in Prison," *Minaret,* January 1996: 24. Ken Baker, "Mike Tyson among Many Who Discover Islam in Prison," *San Jose Mercury News,* May 14, 1994: 10E. Diwan, personal interview. Abdul Hafiz and Jan Diwan, "Prison Da'wah—Issues and Concerns," *Islamic Horizons,* July August 1999: 53; Smith, *Islam in America*, 165. Other ethnicities and nationalities of Muslim prisoners are Latino, Hispanic, Pakistani, Jordanian, Bangladeshi, Indian, and Lebanese.
3. Yawu Miller, "Muslim Minister Settles Suit vs. Suffolk Jail," *Bay State Banner,* 20 March 1997.
4. Abdullah, "Ramadan in Prison," 25. Robert Dannin, "Island in a Sea of Ignorance: Dimensions of the Prison Mosque," *Making Muslim Space in North America and Europe,* ed. Barbara Daly Metcalf (Los Angeles: University of California Press, 1996), 133.
5. Smith, *Islam in America*, 165.
6. Abdullah, "Ramadan in Prison," 25.
7. Mary Rourke, "'It Must Be What Birth Is Like': More Americans Are Experiencing Religious Conversions—and the Hurdles That Can Come with Spiritual Change," *Los Angeles Times,* 22 October 1997: E1.

Chapter 5: Generalizations and Stereotypes: Muslims and the American Media

1. Pam Belluck, "Intolerance and an Attempt to Make Amends Unsettle a Chicago Suburb's Muslims," *New York Times*, 10 August 2000: A10.
2. Mary H. Cooper, "Muslims in America," *CQ Researcher*, 30 April 1993: 374.
3. Edward W. Said, *Covering Islam: How the Media and the Experts Determine How We See the Rest of the World* (New York: Vintage Books, 1997), xi.
4. Ibid., xv.
5. Ibid., xxiii.
6. Cooper, "Muslims in America," 366.
7. Aminah Beverly McCloud, *African-American Islam* (New York: Routledge, 1995), 128.
8. Cooper, "Muslims in America," 365.
9. Ralph Blumenthal, "Jersey City Man Is Charged in Bombing of Trade Center after Rented Van Is Traced," *New York Times*, 5 March 1993: A1.
10. Tom Mashberg, "Man Is Held in N.Y. Bombing," *Boston Globe*, 5 March 1993: 1.
11. Gary Pierre-Pierre, "At Mosque, Muslims Protest News Coverage of Bombing," *New York Times*, 21 March 1993: 38.
12. For more in-depth discussion of media coverage of the TWA Flight 800 Crash, see *The Usual Suspects: Media Coverage of the TWA Flight 800 Crash* (Washington, D.C.: Council on American-Islamic Relations, 1997).
13. Robert Marquand and Lamis Andoni, "Muslims Learn to Pull Political Ropes in U.S.," *Christian Science Monitor*, 5 February 1996: 2. Seventy-seven acts were committed by Puerto Ricans, sixteen by radical Jewish groups, and the rest by various Irish, Latin American, Croatian, and Russian terrorists.
14. Ibid., 2.
15. "Oklahoma Conference Confronts Past Mistakes, Offers New Solutions," *Islamic Horizons* November/December 1996: 12.
16. Richard Scheinin, "Arabian Slights," *San Jose Mercury News*, 2 January 1993: 5C.
17. Salam Al-Marayati, "Growing Up Muslim in America: Stereotypes

Defile a Rich Religion," *Atlanta Constitution,* 1 September 1992: A19.

18. Shahid Athar, *Reflections of an American Muslim* (Chicago: KAZI Publications, 1994), 157.

19. Bob Summer, "The Need to Understand Islam," *Publishers Weekly,* 9 May 1994: 31.

20. Cooper, "Muslims in America," 374.

21. Ibid., 365. McCloud, *African-American Islam,* 129.

22. American-Muslim Research Center, *The Status of Muslim Civil Rights in the United States: The Price of Ignorance* (Washington, D.C.: American-Muslim Research Center, 1996), 18.

23. "Muslim Leaders Meet FBI's Western Regional Offices," *Minaret,* October 1996: 14.

24. McCloud, *African-American Islam,* 128.

25. Robert Marquand, "Arab Engineer Becomes Fluent in American," *Christian Science Monitor,* 22 January 1996: 9.

26. Cooper, "Muslims in America," 378.

27. Ibid., 363.

28. "Disk Jockeys Will Apologize for Mosque Incident," *New York Times,* 31 March 1996: 1, 21.

29. "High Level Italy Conference Discusses Anti-Muslim Bias in Media," *Pakistan Link,* 23 August 1996: 16.

30. Richard Bernstein, "A Growing Islamic Presence: Balancing Sacred and Secular," *New York Times,* 2 May 1993: 1, 26. Peter Steinfels, "Muslim Fast in U.S. Holds Difficulties," *New York Times,* 6 March 1992, natl. ed.: A21. *Christian Science Monitor* reporters Robert Marquand and Lamis Andoni wrote a four-part series on Islam in America, beginning on January 22, 1996. To date, their series is the most recent and most comprehensive. Jeffrey Sheler, "Black Muslims: From Fringe to Bedrock," *U.S. News & World Report,* 8 October 1990: 69–71. Richard N. Ostling, "Americans Facing toward Mecca," *Time,* 23 May 1988: 49–50. Sylvester Monroe, "Doing the Right Thing: Muslims Have Become a Welcome Force in Black Neighborhoods," *Time,* 16 April 1990: 22.

31. See Joan Sabree's article on television reporter Jim Lampley's interview of Southern California Muslims. Joan Sabree, "Masjid Felix Bilal: An Oasis in a Desert of Hopelessness," *Muslim Journal,* 2 June 1989: 1, 7. A recent example of a local paper's story on local Muslims is Melissa Da Ponte's article in *The Sherborn TAB:*

Melissa Da Ponte, "A Matter of Faith: Wayland Mosque Draws MetroWest Muslims," *Sherborn TAB,* 4 February 1997: 14.
For more information on Muslims working on improving media views of Islam, see Abu Amal, "Developing Muslim sterotypes," *Islamic Horizons,* March/April 1998: 56; Tasneema Ghazi, "Literature for Muslim Children in the West," *Islamic Horizons,* May/June 2000: 58–59; "Vigilance Pays," *Message,* July 1996: 11. About the CIE specifically, see Smith, *Islam in America*; Munir Shaikh, "Partners for a Better Education," *Islamic Horizons,* May/June 2000: 64–65.

Close-Up: Movie Muslims: Myth versus Reality

1. Sermid D. El Sarraf, "Three Kings and Hollywood," *Minaret,* October 1999: 19.
2. "Executive Bad Decision," *Message International,* March 1996: 11.
3. Richard Scheinin, "Arabian Slights," *San Jose Mercury News,* 2 January 1993: 5C. See also Mr. Shaheen's latest article, "Hollywood Reel Arabs and Muslims, in *Muslims and Islamization in North America: Problems and Prospects,* ed. Amber Haque.
4. Margaret R. Miles, *Seeing and Believing: Religion and Value in the Movies* (Boston: Beacon Press, 1996), 75.
5. Ibid., 71.
6. Ibid., 72–73.
7. Martin Peretz, "Siege Mentality," *New Republic,* 30 November 1998: 62; Rashad Hussain, "Secret Evidence Bill Must Be Repealed to Preserve Democracy," *Minaret,* July/August 2000: 21.
8. Laurie Goodstein, "Hollywood Now Plays Cowboys and Arabs," *New York Times,* 1 November 1998: 17; Moin Khan, "Hollywood is Unrelenting in Islamophobia," *Islamic Horizons,* January/February 1999: 30.
9. Scheinin, "Arabian Slights," 1C.
10. Lines 5–6, as quoted, were changed but "barbaric" as a description of home remained.
11. Mary H. Cooper, "Muslims in America," *CQ Researcher,* 30 April: 366.
12. Jack G. Shaheen, "Disney: The Purveyor of Racist Images," *Islamic Horizons,* November/December 1996: 26.
13. Shaheen, "Disney: The Purveyor of Racist Images," 26.
14. See Alan Cowell, "The Test of German Tolerance," *New York*

Times, 15 September 1996: 4, 6. For open letter by prominent members of Hollywood community criticizing Germany's treatment of Scientologists, see Frank Rich, "Show Me the Money," *New York Times,* 25 January 1997: 1, 23.
15. Shaheen, "Disney: The Purveyor of Racist Images," 26.
16. Miles, *Seeing and Believing,* 76.

Chapter 6: American Muslim Women: Between Two Worlds

1. "Women in Islam," Islamic Council of New England Conference. Durham, New Hampshire, 5 October 1996.
2. Jane I. Smith, "Islam," *Women in World Religions,* ed. Arvind Sharma (Albany: SUNY Press, 1987), 247.
3. Aminah Beverly McCloud, *African-American Islam,* (New York: Routledge 1995), 147.
4. Smith, "Islam," 249.
5. Yvonne Yazbeck Haddad, *Contemporary Islam and the Challenge of History* (Albany: SUNY Press, 1982), 54.
6. Smith, "Islam," 238, 239, 236.
7. A Muslim woman could only inherit half as much money as a man could because a man was expected to contribute at least half of his inheritance to family needs. A woman's money was her own and was therefore not expected to be used toward family expenses.
8. Jamal Badawi, *Gender Equity in Islam: Basic Principles* (Plainfield, Ind.: American Trust Publications, 1995).
9. Saleem Kayani, *Status of Woman in Islam* (Jamaica, N.Y.: Islamic Circle of North America, 1996).
10. See Marcia K. Hermansen, "The Female Hero in the Islamic Religious Tradition," *The Annual Review of Women in World Religions* II (1992): 111–143.
11. Zehra Panjvani, "Women in Islam," Islamic Council of New England Conference, Durham, New Hampshire, 5 October 1996.
12. Marlise Simons, "Cry of Muslim Women for Equal Rights Is Rising," *New York Times,* 9 March 1998: A1.
13. Rifaat Hassan, "Women in the Context of Change and Confrontation within Muslim Communities," *Women of Faith in Dialogue,* ed. Virginia Ramey Mollenkott (New York: Crossroad, 1987), 98.

14. Carol L. Anway, *Daughters of Another Path* (Lee's Summit, Mo.: Yawna Publications, 1996), 7.
15. Ibid., 116. McCloud, *African-American Islam*, 98.
16. Yvonne Yazbeck Haddad and Adair T. Lummis, *Islamic Values in the United States: A Comparative Study* (New York: Oxford University Press, 1987), 147.
17. Hassan, "Women in the Context of Change and Confrontation within Muslim Communities," 108.
18. Kathleen Gough, "The Origin of Family," *Toward an Anthropology of Women,* ed. Rayna Reiter (New York: Monthly Review Press, 1975), 69–70.
19. Marianne Ferguson, *Women and Religion* (Englewood Cliffs, N.J.: Prentice Hall, 1995), 113.
20. Louis Farrakhan, *A Torchlight for America* (Chicago: FCN Publishing, 1993), 59.
21. Richard Abdus-Saboor, "America's Impact on the Muslim Family," *Muslim Journal,* 19 January 1990: 9.
22. "Voices of the Faithful," *Scholastic Update,* 22 October 1993: 18.
23. Anway, *Daughters of Another Path,* 99.
24. Barbara Crossette, "Women's Rights Gaining Attention within Islam," *New York Times,* 12 May 1996: A3.
25. Ibid.
26. Diego Ribadeneira, "Questions on the Koran: Some Islamic Women Challenge Interpretations They Say Have Hurt Their Gender," *Boston Globe,* 15 January 1997: A1. Ribadeneira's article is an excellent overview of the Islamic feminist dialogue.
27. Ibid., A12.
28. See Shahid Athar, *Reflections of an American Muslim* (Chicago: KAZI Publications, 1994), 32. Muzammil H. Siddiqi, "Issues and Questions," *Pakistan Link,* 8 November 1996: A17.
29. *The Koran Interpreted,* trans. A.J. Arberry (New York: Macmillan Publishing, 1955) 106.
30. Kamran Memon, "Wife Abuse in the Muslim Community," *Islamic Horizons,* March/April 1993: 14.
31. Smith, "Islam," 236.
32. Hassan, "Women in the Context of Change and Confrontation within Muslim Communities," 98, 102, 104, 105. For a positive male view, see "Muslims in the Next Millenium: A Vision for the Future," by Murad Wilfried Hofmann, *Islamic Horizons,* January/February 1999: 22.

33. M. Riaz Khan, "Domestic Violence: American Muslim Families Not Immune," *Islamic Horizons,* July/August 1995: 29.
34. Memon, "Wife Abuse in the Muslim Community," 12.
35. Apna Ghar, *Program for Tapestries in the Looms of Time* (Chicago: Apna Ghar, 1997).
36. Niswa Association, *Niswa Association Pamphlet* (Lomita, Calif.: Niswa Association, 1997).
37. Niswa Association, *Niswa Association Mission Statement* (Lomita, Calif.: Niswa Association, 1996). A similar organization called the Housing Outreach for Muslim Sisters (HOMS) in Arlington, Texas focuses on housing homeless Muslim women and their children. See Michelle Al-Nasr, "Sheltering Homeless Muslims," *Islamic Horizons*, March/April 2000: 44–45.
38. Shahmim Ibrahim, personal interview, 14 August 1996.
39. Najma Adam, personal interview, 21 September 1996.
40. Memon, "Wife Abuse in the Muslim Community," 12.
41. Ibid., 14.
42. Ibid., 16.
43. Najma Adam, personal interview.
44. Shahmim Ibrahim, personal interview. Najma Adam, personal interview.
45. Memon, "Wife Abuse in the Muslim Community," 16.
46. Louise Cainkar, "Palestinian Women in American Society: The Interaction of Social Class, Culture and Politics," in *The Development of Arab-American Identity,* ed. Ernest McCarus (Ann Arbor: University of Michigan Press, 1994) 100. Beverly Thomas McCloud, "African-American Muslim Women," in *The Muslims of America,* ed. Yvonne Yazbeck Haddad (New York: Oxford University Press, 1991), 182.
47. For free medical clinics founded and run by Muslims, see "Muslims Serving Humanity," *Islamic Horizons*, May/June 2000: 13 about Al-Shifa Free Clinic; "The only Good Alternative," *Muslim Magazine*, Spring 1999: 64–65 about "Stepping Together"; Silveen Khan, "Texan Muslims Focus on Social Services," *Islamic Horizons*, May/June 1998: 30–31 about the Muslim Community Center for Human Services; Ernest Tucker, "Muslim doctors live their faith," *Chicago Sun Times*, 2 September 2000: 4.
48. Anway, *Daughters of Another Path,* 85–86. Melissa Da Ponte, "A Matter of Faith: Wayland Mosque Draws MetroWest Muslims," *Sherborn TAB,* 4 February 1997: 14.

Close-Up: The Long Road for Female Converts to Islam

1. Carol Anway, *Daughters of Another Path* (Lee's Summit, Mo.: Yawna Publications, 1996), 56; other stories on pp. 173, 147, 53–54.

Close-Up: *Hijab* In America: Why Won't Westerners Understand?

1. Aminah Beverly McCloud, *African-American Islam* (New York: Routledge, 1995), 143. Karen Armstrong also subscribes to this view.

Chapter 7: Growing Up in America: Creating New World Islam

1. Nadia Amri, "The Gateway to Information," *Islamic Horizons*, May/June 2000: 52; Wafa Khorshid, "Islamic Virtual School," *Islamic Horizons*, May/June 1998: 38.
2. Warren Hoge, "Bradford Journal: Marked for Death, by Their Families," *New York Times,* 18 October 1997: A4.

Close-Up: Whither Reform Islam? What American Muslims Can Learn from American Jews

1. Craig Horowitz, "The Disappearance of American Jews," *New York,* 14 July 1997: 33.
2. Ibid., 32.

Close Up: Full-Time Islamic Schools: Making Growing Up Muslim in America Easier

1. Yvonne Yazbeck Haddad and Adair T. Lummis, *Islamic Values in the United States: A Comparative Study* (New York: Oxford

University Press, 1987), 49. Susan Sachs, "Muslim Schools in U.S. a Voice for Identity," *New York Times*, 10 November 1998: B10. Riaz Khan, "Averting Teenage Temptations," *Islamic Horizons,* May/June 1996: 29, 31. Carol Anway found in her study that 26 percent of American Muslim mothers sent their children to full-time Islamic schools: Carol Anway, *Daughters of Another Path* (Lee's Summit, Mo.: Yawna Publications, 1996).

2. New Horizon School, *Mission Statement* (Los Angeles: New Horizon School, 1997).

3. Fazlur Rahman, *Islam and Modernity* (Chicago: University of Chicago Press, 1982), 53.

4. Louise Cainkar, "Palestinian Women in American Society: The Interaction of Social Class, Culture and Politics," in *The Development of Arab-American Identity,* ed. Ernest McCarus (Ann Arbor: University of Michigan Press, 1994), 93.

5. Rahman, *Islam and Modernity,* 78.

6. Peter Steinfels, "Muslim Fast in U.S. Holds Difficulties," *New York Times,* 6 March 1992: A21. Public schools, however are increasingly trying to accommodate Muslim students on an administrative level. Somini Sengupta, "Ramadan Enters New York City School Life," *New York Times,* 6 February 1997: A1.

7. Anis Ahmed, personal interview, 17 January 1997. Students at the New Horizon school had various ethnicities: African-American, Bangladeshi, Bosnian, German, Indian, Iraqi, Pakistani, Saudi-Arabian, and Syrian among many others. Daa'iyah Ahmad included in this list Asian, European-American, and Somalian. Daa'iyah Ahmad, personal interview, 7 March 1997.

8. Gasser Hathout, *"Juma* Prayer," New Horizon School, Los Angeles, 17 January 1997. Muslims consider Friday as their holy day.

9. Sonsyrea Tate, *Little X: Growing Up in the Nation of Islam* (New York: HarperSanFrancisco, 1997), 77, 208.

10. One boy, the son of Bangladeshi immigrants, had previously attended a "magnet" public school, a school for gifted children enrolled in public school. One can presume that the student body at magnet public schools is more manageable and less likely to participate in subversive behavior than those of non-magnet public schools.

11. Various students, personal interview, 17 January 1997.

Chapter 8: Muslims and American Politics: Creating Unity from the Inside Out

1. Ali A. Mazrui, "Between the Crescent and the Star-Spangled Banner: American Muslims and U.S. Foreign Policy," *International Affairs* 72.3 (1996): 498. Yvonne Yazbeck Haddad and Adair T. Lummis, *Islamic Values in the United States: A Comparative Study* (New York: Oxford University Press, 1987), 102. Muslim Public Affairs Council, *Press Release: Report on Polling of Muslim Voters* (Los Angeles: Muslim Public Affairs Council, 1996).
2. Jeffrey L. Sheler, "Islam in America" *U.S. News & World Report*, 8 October 1990: 71.
3. Mazrui, "Between the Crescent and the Star-Spangled Banner," 493.
4. Steven A. Johnson, "Political Activity of Muslims in America," *The Muslims of America,* ed. Yvonne Yazbeck Haddad (New York: Oxford, 1991), 115.
5. Ibid., 118.
6. Robert Marquand and Lamis Andoni, "Muslims Learn to Pull Political Ropes in U.S.," *Christian Science Monitor,* 5 February 1996: 12.
7. Ramadan Alig, "Seeking their Due," *Islamic Horizons,* March/April 2000: 48. See Jocelyn Y. Stewart, "A Milestone for Muslims," *Los Angeles Times*, 28 January 1998: B1.
8. Paul Merrion, "Flying High—With the President on Air Force One," *Pakistan Link,* 23 August 1996: 23.
9. Gasser Hathout, *The American-Muslim Foreign Policy Perspective* (Los Angeles: Muslim Public Affairs Council, 1996), 2.
10. Muzammil Ahmed, "Media, War and the Making of Consent," *Message,* March 1991: 16.
11. Robert Marquand, "U.S. Muslims Feel Constant Tug of Events around the World," *Christian Science Monitor,* 5 February 1996: 10.
12. Muslim Public Affairs Council, *Press Release: Report on Polling of Muslim Voters.* Salam Al-Marayati, "Why Do We Need the Muslim Vote," *Minaret,* October 1999: 21.
13. Majority of ISNA Members are Voters," *Islamic Horizons* November/December 1996: 11.
14. Mazrui, "Between the Crescent and the Star-Spangled Banner" 493–506.

15. Marquand and Andoni, "Muslims Learn to Pull Political Ropes in U.S.," 12. Muslim Public Affairs Council, *Program: Muslim Public Affairs Council and Muslim Women's' League Honor First Lady Hillary Rodham Clinton* (Los Angeles: Muslim Public Affairs Council, 1996), 2.
16. "An Interview with the Clinton/Gore Campaign," *Minaret,* October 1996: 25.
17. Marquand and Andoni, "Muslims Learn to Pull Political Ropes in U.S.," 10.
18 Muslim Public Affairs Council, *Press Release: Report on Polling of Muslim Voters.*
19. Muslim Public Affairs Council, *Issues '96: A Political Agenda Published by the Muslim Public Affairs Council* (Los Angeles: Muslim Public Affairs Council, 1996).
20. Abu Amal Hadhrami, "Muslims Struggle for Equality," *Islamic Horizons,* March/April 1999: 58; Khadijah Binti Abdullah, "Establishing Muslim Holidays," *Islamic Horizons,* May/June 1999: 51.

Chapter 10: Where American Islam Is Going

1. For examples of anti-Islamic sentiment in Europe, see the following articles: Patrick Sookhedo, "Prince Charles Is Wrong: Islam Does Menace the West," *Daily Telegraph,* 19 December 1996: 20. Norma Claire Moruzzi, "A Problem with Headscarves: Contemporary Complexities of Political and Social Identity," *Political Theory* 22.4 (1994): 665. Ali B. Mazrui, "Between the Crescent and the Star-Spangled Banner: American Muslims and Foreign Policy," *International Affairs* 72.3 (1996): 502.
2. Barbara D. Metcalf, "Introduction: Sacred Words, Sanctioned Practice, New Communities," *Making Muslim Space in North America and Europe,* ed. Barbara Daly Metcalf (Los Angeles: University of California Press, 1996), 2.

INDEX